MEETING
DAVE

a journey through the looking glass

Pamela Voccia PhD

Table Of Contents

Chapter One – page 1
Through the Looking Glass

Chapter Two – page 8
Releasing the Jabberwocky

Chapter Three – page 34
The Mad Hatter

Chapter Four – page 58
Off With Their Heads

Chapter Five – page 69
Curiouser and Curiouser

Chapter Six – page 74
Drink Me

Chapter Seven – page 82
Mad Tea Party

Chapter Eight – page 88
Painting the Roses Red

Chapter Nine – page 108
Down the Rabbit Hole

Chapter Ten – page 140
Cheshire Smiles

Chapter Eleven – page 160
Return to Wonderland

Chapter Twelve – page 166
Eggshells

For Mom

Chapter One
<u>Through the Looking Glass</u>

The White Rabbit put on his spectacles.
"Where shall I begin, please your Majesty?" he asked.
"Begin at the beginning,"
the King said, very gravely,
"and go on till you come to the end: then stop."

— *Lewis Carroll, Alice's Adventures in Wonderland, Chapter 12*

He asked me to help him.

I am his big sister after all. He doesn't know that I don't have the answers, because I have always had the answers. I was always farther along than he, and he could never catch up. He saw me as an over-achiever. Successful. Normal. Everything he wasn't.

Sibling rivalry among children with varying talents can be more intense than in other families. I don't know why; I haven't looked into it. I think it may be because some gifts are appreciated by those around us, and some are not. I don't know.

My brother asked me to help him…. So, I said I would.

I've spent a whole life following my instincts, and it has served me well so far. I just get things done.
I set out to accomplish something impossible, and then I just do, somehow. Maybe because it wasn't really impossible – just statistically unlikely.

I operate on intuition and I don't typically have a plan … I just go with my gut and it works.

I can accomplish this, too… although I have no idea how.

My brother asked me to help him, and all of a sudden, I believed I could. I could finally help him out of the darkness, once and for all.

My brother killed himself on Thursday, June 29th, 2017. That is the date on his death certificate, but I knew he was gone on Monday, 3 days before – because I no longer felt his darkness.

I went to work on Tuesday and said to my co-workers, "Something's wrong."

On Wednesday, I said to them, "I think my brother is dead," and I started looking at bereavement time. On Thursday I was driving home from work and I called my son, Quentin. He said, "Mom, grandma is making BLTs for dinner. Also, she can't talk to you right now and she didn't let me call you at work… but David's dead," and he began to cry. Quentin has autism – but somehow, his delivery was spot on.

I knew my brother was gone on Monday, or at least in a coma. No one heard from him after that. If he had been conscious, he wouldn't have been able to stop himself from sending a nasty message to my parents. He was angry with them. When he was in the pit, he lashed out.

So, my journey began when he asked me to help him. It began the minute I heard him say the words. They were loud and clear.

He reached out for the first time in 25 years and asked me for help - one week after he died.

I was in my room, listening to the fireworks outside. Fourth of July in Florida goes on for a week…. Boom Boom Boom. I didn't have the television on. I was just lying there, listening, watching the rockets' red glare on my walls.

And suddenly, I felt my brother there. He wasn't coming forward, like the others tend to do…. but I knew he was there.

2

I finally said, breaking the silence, "Are you ok, David?"

He said, "It's dark here."

I said, "You were supposed to go into the light..."

"There is no light," he finally said.

"There is, David. You just forgot how to see it," I told him.

Then he said, "Can you help me?"

And I said I would.

I said I would before I knew how. I said I would because I'm his older sister and I'm supposed to be able to fix things. I said I would because my little brother was emerging from the darkness and he needed my help. I said I would because he still believed I was smarter and stronger and could do more... and that I was always one step ahead. I said I would because, all of a sudden, I believed I could help him.

So, I went on a pilgrimage to help him find his light.

For many years, I had thought about writing a clinical book about borderline personality disorder from a family's perspective. After my brother died, I realized I had to.... but the story changed - it took a different path. It went down the rabbit hole. I began feeling like Alice in Wonderland, incredulous at what was transpiring around me; experiencing what it is like to question if your own perceptions are real.

For someone perceived as normal, I've had my share of paranormal experiences as well. I've encountered situations that are not easily explained by science and reason - and those experiences were part of this experience, as well. I thought about not including them in this book, out of concern for alienating readers... but everything that has

transpired - the physical, the metaphysical, and the emotional – all
are part of this story,

It all needs to be told … if any of it is told.

My brother posted his multiple suicide attempts on social media. He
openly ranted for decades. He wanted everyone to know how much
he was suffering when he was alive.

And finally, I can help him.

And, so, let's begin.

****

July 2, 2017
Facebook post on Hues of Dave memorial page:

I am David's big sister and I have something to say...
David and I were best friends growing up... we found ourselves
alone in new and strange environments and we relied on each other.
We moved from New York state to Canada in elementary school. We
made it work. We then moved to Florida when I was in high school
and he was in middle school ... We got SeaWorld passes and went
every weekend because we had no friends here- but we had a blast!
The first baby Shamu was born that year and we went every
weekend to see her (or him?)

I got into my first rear-end collision taking him to get ice cream after
his appendectomy... and we were afraid to tell Mom because he
wasn't wearing his seatbelt
because it rubbed on the incision/ stiches.

We scripted and staged performances featuring our pets.
Comedic gold!
If only we'd had the technology back then to record it....

We took long road trips together to New York to see our
grandmother and we sang and laughed the whole way.

And.... I believe I was the first Target of his Madness.
One day, out of the blue, he hated me.
I was his enemy and I didn't know why.

I remember the moment my "brother" was gone forever.
I remember very distinctly going to dinner for his birthday and he
brought a friend, and his new girlfriend, and after dinner I gave him
a gift and he looked at me like a venomous stranger and said to me,
"I don't want your gift. You treated me like shit my whole life."

I was confused. My parents were confused. His hatred was palpable. Everyone in the room was uncomfortable ... so my boyfriend at the time tried to lighten the mood and said, "Well David, that's a really expensive gift so whatever she did, I'm sure it makes up for it."
You could have heard a pin drop
.... forever.
It was a downward spiral from then on.

Yes, I believe I was the first person that the Madness hated. Shortly thereafter, the Madness hated my father - again no one knows why. Then long-standing best friends started to drop like flies. I'm sure the Madness had stories and excuses, but the reality is:
the Madness is Darkness.
It lies and consumes.
It's death.

I already mourned my brother, or so I thought. I lost my brother over 20 years ago - and I never again connected to the man in the aging David suit who would show up every once in a while.
But when the Madness took its own spiteful, tragic life, it took my little brother with it and I now I truly, deeply mourn.

I had a little brother once and, as you've all attested, he was funny. He was brilliant, too.... And I'm so, so, so sorry that I couldn't reach the sadness and anger inside.
I think, after a while, I was too angry to even try...
So, I didn't try.

I also think that maybe, as a boy, David's young heart was SO big that it was just too susceptible to the pain and darkness that lurks in the shadows...

The Madness would be so angry at me for saying this, but this is for the beautiful soul that passed on:
My little brother had Michael Jackson posters on his walls and every Star Wars figure in the world. When he was little, he ran around in Underoos and always had a blanket tied around his neck as a "cape".

6

He won a giant stuffed bear at Darien Lake once and gave it to me
because I was sad that I couldn't win one... but he was never, ever
able to win another one for himself...
Not ever.
And THAT's the metaphor.

We had joy and laughter for many cherished years,
until one day the laughter stopped.
For those of you who relate, thank you for loving him once,
and my family wishes you peace.

****

Chapter Two
<u>Releasing the Jabberwocky</u>

Alice: "It's RATHER hard to understand!"

*(You see she didn't like to confess, even to herself,
that she couldn't make it out at all.)*

*"Somehow it seemed to fill my head with ideas
- only I don't know exactly what they are!
However, SOMEBODY killed SOMETHING:
that's clear, at any rate"*

-Lewis Carroll, Through the Looking Glass – Chapter 1

How do you write a story that begins at the end? That was my initial question. My brother is dead. His story is over – so the climax of the book occurs before it starts.

Those were my initial thoughts.

I was wrong. The journey was just beginning.

For 30 years I watched a borderline from afar. After he finally succeeded in killing himself, I was going to write a book about borderline personality disorder from the family perspective: as a psychologist and a sister and a daughter in a family that has been irrevocably changed by the disorder.

I intended to share our story in an effort to provide insight to families of people suffering with borderline personality disorder. I wanted to write something for clinicians, in order to expand their understanding of what the family experience of borderline personality disorder really is. So many of us are locked into the old definitions, which describe the disorder as being created by abusive or dysfunctional families, mimicking bipolar disorder in symptomatology, yet not responding to meds. I wanted to provide an account from the other side of the looking glass.

This was never intended to be a biography of David. I don't have the right or the authority to pen that.

Or the inclination....

I really didn't know the man he had become. In the end, we had been separated by decades of separate lives - and over these decades, I felt like Alice standing alone, having professional tantrums from a thousand miles away, while year after year he was mis-diagnosed and mis-medicated. "Drink Me"... "Take Me"... bottle after bottle, but yet nothing helped. He was a borderline. The bottles and pills weren't going to help with what he was suffering from... and they didn't. As he descended further and further into Madness, I was helpless. Surely, I couldn't be the only person in Wonderland who could see what was happening? I was frustrated and angry, and I hated him for the pain he was causing my parents.

Writing about my brother's borderline personality disorder may seem like a violation of privacy, but everyone he knew is aware that he killed himself, and most people knew that he had made multiple suicide attempts. This was not a secret. Close family and friends weren't left to wonder, "Why?" We knew why; he wanted to die. The likelihood of his eventual death from suicide was our reality.

There were some people on the periphery who were left to wonder "why" – as much from his actions in life as in death – so this book also began as an effort to answer the "why" for the people who are left suffering, as much as to help those who may be suffering now, in their own families. An effort to make David's life and death matter, because his story deserves to be told...

It's an important story. It's an important message: the darkness comes, and it takes everything, and it's contagious - and the survivors are left to cope with grief and anger and confusion and guilt.

It's a story that needs to be told because most people don't know what borderline personality disorder is, and it killed my little brother.

Borderlines: What you don't know could kill them

"Really, now you ask me,"
said Alice, very much confused,
"I don't think—"

"Then you shouldn't talk," said the Hatter.

Lewis Carroll, Alice's Adventures in Wonderland – Chapter 7

The National Institute of Mental Health (NIMH) describes borderline personality disorder as:

> "a mental illness marked by an ongoing pattern of varying moods, self-image, and behavior. These symptoms often result in impulsive actions and problems in relationships. People with borderline personality disorder may experience intense episodes of anger, depression, and anxiety that can last from a few hours to days" (2018).

People suffering from borderline personality disorder experience symptoms such as excessive anger – known as borderline rage – paranoia, negative self-image, intense fears of abandonment, chronic emptiness, impulsive self-harm and mood lability. These symptoms are typically the result of some external factor – something perceived in a social interaction (or lack thereof) – rather than internally triggered.

The current DSM-V diagnostic criteria for borderline personality disorder states that the essential features of borderline personality disorder include impairments in self- and interpersonal functioning.

Impairments in self functioning include an unstable self-image, excessive self-criticism, chronic feelings of emptiness, and lack of self-direction.

Impairments in interpersonal functioning include a lack of empathy or ability to recognize feelings or needs of others, hypersensitivity, the tendency to feel slighted or insulted, intense unstable relationships marked by mistrust, fears of abandonment, and alternating between idealization and devaluation of the partner.

Pathological personality traits in the following areas are also required for diagnosis of borderline personality disorder:

- Negative Affectivity (emotional lability, reactions that are disproportionate to the circumstance, anxiety, fears of rejection, loss of autonomy, feelings of shame, hopelessness, difficulty recovering from feeling down, thoughts of suicide.)
- Disinhibition: (impulsivity, difficulty establishing or following plans, self-harming behavior under emotional distress, engaging in potentially harmful activities, unnecessarily and without regard to or understanding of the reality of personal danger.)
- Antagonism: (persistent or frequent anger or irritability in response to minor slights and insults)

Adapted from The Diagnostic and Statistical Manual of Mental Disorders -V

Part of the tragedy is that there is no "cure"; no drug to take the disorder away. Borderline personality disorder is the only psychiatric disorder for which the primary intervention is psychosocial (Gunderson 2009). There are currently no FDA approved medications indicated for the treatment of borderline personality disorder. There is treatment – but the answer is for the person to acknowledge and fully comprehend that they have distorted perceptions, and that they are continuing to create victimization in their own minds.

Asking them to look at their own experience of perceived, ongoing trauma and maltreatment and to realize that, regardless of the past, moving forward *they* are the ones causing their own problems …

that's handing them a cake marked "Eat Me", and expecting them to
now function in Upside-down world.

The appropriate clinical phrase is "person with Borderline
Personality Disorder." Those of us trying to cope with it just tend to
use the term, "borderline" – mostly as a descriptor of how it feels to
experience the disorder, from all sides: Living on the borderline of
irrational behavior; bordering on pulling the last straw; teetering on
the edge of the border wall. And loved ones often find ourselves
pushed to the borderline of either giving up or breaking down.

The term "borderline" has become a colloquialism – and according
to Dr. John Gunderson (who is widely credited as the father of the
Borderline Personality Disorder diagnosis), the term has earned its
status as an accurate descriptor of the disorder's unclear and flexible
boundaries (Gunderson 2009). The descriptor is a question mark.
"*Borderline* (is) an adjective searching for a noun" (Akiskal 1985).

I have had numerous personal experiences with borderlines – and
most of the symptoms I reference come from my observations and
experiences with them.

Borderlines often make numerous suicide attempts, and many
eventually succeed. For each of those suicides, there are those close
by, as well as those far away in time or distance, who are hit with the
suicide shrapnel and knocked out of commission for a moment… or
for a while… or for life.

We become the walking wounded – with holes in us, caused by
trauma, that will never completely heal. Survivors of borderline
suicides are like war veterans – because, in truth, we've spent years
in the trenches - except we never had a fighting chance.

Current theory has moved away from an environmental cause of
borderline personality disorder, toward a hereditary one. Current
research indicates up to 60% heritability of the disorder (Gunderson
2011) with emergence of clinical symptomatology in late
adolescence through early adulthood.

Borderlines are oversensitive to perceived slights from others. They are emotionally labile and impulsive in their desire to retaliate or overcorrect a perceived insult. They rarely feel loved *enough*.

A common descriptor for borderlines: Bottomless pits of need. It is like they have a hole in them, and any love or attention poured into them from external sources just runs out like sand in an hourglass - and they can't seem to remember what it felt like to be full for those brief moments, before everything turned upside down and the sand started running out again.

Ironically, it is often they who turn their own worlds upside down. For the most part, it does no good to point that out to a borderline, however. They won't see it. To them we're the ones in Upside-down world, not them.

As with most disorders, functionality depends on the severity of the case, and the inherent capability of the individual. Recovery would likely depend on functionality, as well. In general, borderlines are able to do one or two things well, or very well if they're very interested in a topic or an art form, but generally are unable to hold down a job, to advance a career, or sustain long term relationships. As a result, they can become a drain on family finances or recipients of welfare, which can further affect their feelings of guilt and self-loathing.

The borderlines I have encountered love animals - especially dogs. Pets may be the only thing that can give them the level of constant, excessive love and affection which helps them (temporarily) feel full, while it is all the while running out the hole in the bottom. Dogs certainly give unconditional positive regard. Dogs don't hold grudges. No matter how they are treated, dogs reset and are ready to be your best friend again, the moment the storm is over.

People, aren't as forgiving - we can't pour enough attention into a borderline to keep them alive and still maintain a life of our own. While we take a minute to put on our own oxygen masks, they have slipped away from us in an abandoned rage.

14

Borderlines are terrified of abandonment – so much so that they will push people away, convinced they will leave them eventually, anyhow. This may be a way of taking control of the inevitable pain they believe they will feel, much like cutting may be a way of taking control of the emotional pain they invariably feel. Withholding – or not giving enough of one's self – appears to be one of the worst offenses perceived by a borderline. If you don't answer the phone, or cancel plans, a borderline can perceive this withholding of attention or affection as a direct attack – and respond accordingly. Their retaliation will often be perceived by the recipient to be disproportionate to the incident – but a borderline is convinced that they are responding in kind. Borderline rage is often a reaction to the perception that a significant person is withholding, uncaring or abandoning them. (Berenson, 2011)

In all of the cases with which I am personally familiar, illegal drug use severely exacerbated borderline symptoms… and borderlines are often drawn to drugs. Borderlines are constantly searching for ways to ease the pain inside, and sedative drugs and alcohol may be soothing. Long term drug and alcohol abuse, however, seems to impair the frontal lobe, leading to an impaired ability to rationally interpret or react to perceived threat.

I believe that people who are enablers – unwittingly playing into the disorder – can exacerbate the Madness by buying into the stories of abuse. They can reinforce the borderline's feelings of being abused or neglected; of not having their needs met by family or significant others. Borderline personality disorder is like pathological selfishness, and if it is fed into, like anything else, it grows.

Most borderlines (>70%) report a history of abuse (Gunderson 2009). For many years, abuse was considered to be a precursor to development of borderline personality disorder. A number of borderlines report being sexually abused as children. However, it is currently estimated that up to 45 percent of borderlines have no history of such abuse (New 2008)

In addition, 80 percent of people who were abused as children do NOT develop borderline personality disorder (New 2008). Therefore, it appears that childhood abuse is not necessarily a cause of borderline personality disorder, but may simply be an accelerating factor in a genetically predisposed individual.

For many borderlines, there may not have been actual abuse, as much as there was their perception of being abused. I've personally come to the conclusion that borderlines invariably claim abuse because normal human interaction actually *feels* abusive to them. They perceive imaginary slights, and this is their reality.

This is not to discount the experience of those who were actually abused. If a person who is neurologically predisposed to borderline traits is actually abused, the disorder appears to be exacerbated to the point of disfunction at an accelerated pace - which is perhaps why this group was the first to catch the eye of psychiatry.

For a borderline, a person is either light (idealized) or dark (devalued) – there is no grey area. You cannot be a good person who has inadvertently hurt them through carelessness, mis-intention, or acts of common human frailty.

If you are a person of light, they will do anything for you. Once you go dark, however, you are flawed and not to be trusted. You are the enemy: to be berated, retaliated against or cut out of their lives completely.

Confronting a borderline is like throwing holy water on a vampire. Presenting them with a reality that their *own perceptions* are distorted is something that they often will not face. Many borderlines will not even entertain it, even during the initial course of counseling therapy that they, themselves, sought out. Typically, when they do get in front of someone who finally understands what they're dealing with, the borderline will discontinue the sessions because it doesn't support their victim identity.

According to my friend, Kelly, who is a clinical psychologist: "Cognitive behavior (CBT) based techniques can often backfire very quickly with patients who have personality disorders. Dependent upon the statements and behaviors of the therapist, if the person with BPD does not feel 'understood', they may end treatment.

Many therapists make the mistake of not spending enough time getting to know the BPD patient, and therefore do not show the necessary empathy for that patient's 'world.' The patient is not convinced that the therapist 'gets it.' Instead, the therapist relies on the usual CBT-based techniques that question the patient's thinking or suggest the patient can change things.

These challenges may feel too destabilizing to the patient, affectively, and the therapist can be perceived as not understanding - therefore a threat. My view is that timing is everything in therapy, more so with people with personality disorders than Axis I disorders, and the right to challenge the patient's world has to be earned in a different way than with patients with Axis I disorders than Axis II disorders... and you can cite me for this entire paragraph..." (2018)

Unfortunately, many borderlines don't even reach that point in treatment. They are often misdiagnosed as bipolar and pharmacologically treated as such. The meds, which were developed to correct chemical imbalances do not address the personality disorder. Insurance companies traditionally would not pay for therapeutic treatment of borderlines, because there weren't outcome-based treatment measures.

As a result, psychologists, counselors and psychiatrists would have to provide another diagnosis – one for which the patient also met criteria, such as bipolar, anxiety or major depressive disorder – and when the patient invariably left the practitioner who was getting too close to solving the puzzle, and jumped ship to another therapist, the progress reset itself, once again.

Jumping ship is an appropriate analogy. Their preservation of self seems to rely on maintaining a victim identity, and the validation of perceived slights as external to them. Losing that identity would be losing that self: a death, in itself. When the lifeboat is taking them too far from the disorder, they jump off, back into the dark water - to flail, once again...alone.

Dr. Gunderson, a professor at Harvard University, contributed to the original diagnostic classification criteria in the Diagnostic and Statistical Manual of Mental Disorders (DSM-III) in 1980. Any practitioner who has studied this disorder likely has at least one book authored by Dr. Gunderson on their bookshelf. (I did, I just hadn't read it yet).

The Gunderson clinic at McLean Hospital in Massachusetts is one of the handful in the country that has met success in treating borderline personality disorder.

My guess is that these individuals were motivated to change – and came to the situation with a workable level of self-awareness. I truly don't believe that my brother was in that workable place, at any time, as an adult. I can't imagine the success rate for treatment of borderlines who don't want to do the work involved in therapeutic intervention.

In the late 1980s, Marsha Linehan developed a new treatment, Dialectical Behavioral Therapy (DBT), for the chronically suicidal borderline individual. Within this modality, "dialectical" refers to the multiple tensions that coexist within the borderline patient (Linehan 1987). DBT seeks to replace maladaptive behaviors with coping skills such as mindfulness and distress tolerance, and is currently the only empirically supported treatment for borderline personality disorder (May 2016).

The history of the identification of Borderline Personality Disorder is fascinating. The following is summarized from *An Interview with John Gunderson on Borderline Personality Disorder* by Signume Karterud in Oslo, Norway. (Video copyright UiO 2015):

In the 1970s, the field of psychiatry was dominated by psychoanalysis, but there was a group of people presenting for treatment who were driving the practitioners crazy – and they were actually getting worse with psychoanalysis. As an expert in schizophrenia, Dr. Gunderson conducted a literature review in order to further examine these cases of the "borderline schizophrenics." In the interview, he says that he was interested in defining the disorder because these patients literally scared him – and as an empirical hospital researcher, he began wondering where the successful cases were. By the 1980s there were 54 published books on the disorder, but not one documented case of successful treatment.

Dr Gunderson's experience over the past 40 years has led to these findings on the etiological development of the disorder:

- Interpersonal hypersensitivity: a child who is innately over sensitive to interpersonal interaction. (They perceive neglect when a parent frowns or leaves a room)
- Predisposition to emotional control: a child who has excessive, inappropriate responses to situations
- Attachment: may result from poor parenting or from trying to parent a child who is innately difficult. A parent's own vulnerabilities are exacerbated by a child such as this
- Real trauma can contribute to the development of the disorder

In the interview, Dr. Gunderson addressed the issue of the dysfunctional family system of a borderline by acknowledging that decades of practitioners have lamented in the literature about not being able to handle these patients - and they only have to deal with them for one hour per week. He says that it became clear to him that these families were doing the best they could. Borderlines demand your presence and vigilance. "If you blink your eyes, they will notice it!"

I had my staff of master's level clinicians watch the interview. I want to do my part in educating the next generation of clinicians on borderline personality disorder.

Despite its prevalence and potential lethality, borderline personality disorder remains under-funded and under-researched.

Dr. Perry Hoffman, in his presentation for the National Education Alliance for Borderline Personality Disorders, reports that schizophrenia affects 0.4% of the population, and receives 300 million each year for research. Bipolar disorder affects 1.6% of the population, and receives 100 million dollars each year for research. Borderline personality disorder affects 6% of the population – yet only receives 6 million, annually, in research funds (Hoffman 2003).

In the same presentation, he cites the results from a family burden inventory, which looks at how the presence of borderline personality disorder in a family member affects the others in the family:

- Worry about patient's future: 94%
- Intensity of family friction: 87%
- Impact on own ability to concentrate 87%
- Upset household routine: 84%
- Reduced leisure time: 78%
- Fear own behavior makes patient worse: 77%
- Worry how much patient changed: 74%

(Hoffman 2003)

From my personal observations, as well as from my interactions with professionals in the field of psychology over the years, it appears that borderlines are almost invariably institutionalized in some setting during their lifetime: females predominantly in mental wards; males predominantly in drug treatment or jails. Approximately 75% of borderlines attempt suicide, at least once (New 2008). These attempts are often not lethal, but could have resulted in death, given the right circumstances. The completed suicide rate in borderlines is about 10% (New 2008).

Another observation from my personal experience and conversations: Families do not talk about the disorder, which is why people not intimately involved with borderline personality disorder may have no idea what it is. Families of borderlines are suffering, but in silence. "Often devastating, borderline personality disorder is an illness that not only affects the individuals with the diagnosis, but also intensely affects those who care about them." (Gunderson, 2005)

So why do families of borderlines not talk about the disorder?

To begin with, borderlines can be *horrible*. There, I said it. Borderlines can be emotional hijackers, flying into a rage, or using retaliatory "suicide" attempts, in response to perceived slights – with a mantra that seems to be: "I'll show you!"

And it is *horrible* to watch their suffering and not be able to help. Trying to soothe a borderline loved one can be exhausting – and the feelings of helplessness and guilt and fatigue are not something most of us want to talk about with outsiders.
My mother said that one time she did attempt to discuss borderline personality disorder with a friend, but her friend kept misunderstanding it as bipolar disorder – so my mother gave up the conversation. She didn't have the energy or the tools to educate someone else on the disorder – she barely understood it, herself.

Secondly, families don't stop loving one of their own just because they are mentally ill – and talking about it feels like a betrayal. (*Writing* about it feels like a betrayal.) Friends and relatives eventually begin to see that something is very wrong, and out of consideration, stop asking questions.

Let's not forget that there are still some current practitioners who believe the disorder to be caused by abuse or dysfunction in the family - so that stigma alone could preclude anyone from wanting to bring it up.

Practitioners often steer clear of treating borderlines. Why? Because borderlines can be doomsday timebombs – and the pervasive feeling is that nothing good is coming down that pike. On January 19th, 2009, the cover of Time Magazine read, "Borderline Personality: The Disorder That Doctors Fear Most."

Some of my closest friends are practitioners in the field of psychology – and they typically don't look forward to a borderline coming through the doors. (Although they rarely show up as a borderline – it's usually self-diagnosed depression and anxiety that prompts them to seek help, or they come in with a history of "bipolar disorder.")

They require more time than we have, more attention than we can give, and at the end of the day: rage against the notion that their perceptions are at the root of all of their current problems. As Kelly puts it: "Ruminative revenge with that borderline fume of anger… When they're overreacting to misperception of threat and coming from a ruminative mental state, that's a shit show."

Borderlines know that their life is a shit show. They can articulate that. Typically, however, even if they acknowledge that they have overreacted, they claim their outburst was still a reaction to something someone else did. In their minds, the anger or retaliation, itself, wasn't inappropriate – it was justified, even if the response was out of hand.

The following are internet quotes about borderline personality disorder by those suffering from it. It is important to see how they feel about their experience. For the most part, I believe that these would have to be high functioning borderlines, who have a high capacity and inclination toward insight:

- "Having Borderline feels like eternal Hell. Never knowing how I am going to feel from one minute to the next. Hurting because I hurt those who I love"
- "It is hard to be accused of manipulation when it's a scream for love."

- "I keep so much pain inside myself. I grasp my anger and loneliness and hold it in my chest. It has changed me into something I never meant to be. It has transformed me into a person I do not recognize. But I don't know how to let it go."
- "It hurts so bad when you have a fear of abandonment caused by a mental disorder, but it's that same mental disorder that causes people to walk out of your life. (above quotes taken from source: https://www.healthyplace.com/insight/quotes/borderline-personality-disorder-quotes)
- "You know you're borderline when you fluctuate between fearing abandonment to encouraging it." — (Jaen Wirefly https://mybpdstory.wordpress.com/you-know-youre-borderline-when/)

Ironically, it is the behavioral manifestation of the disorder, in itself, that can result in a lack of empathy for those suffering from the disorder. Borderlines can snap in a flash: one moment lucid and normal, and the next, borderline psychotic – dangerously striking out like a cornered animal.

****

When I returned to work after my week of bereavement, I found myself in a breakroom conversation with our research psychiatrist, talking about my brother's recent suicide. I shared with her my belief that he was an untreated borderline who had been misdiagnosed for many years.

Coincidentally, she had just gone to a conference on borderline personality disorder. We work in Alzheimer's research – finding out that she had just been to a talk on borderline personality disorder was surprising… timely.

Serendipitous…

There were many incidences in my journey following my brother's death where I was surprised to find myself in front of exactly the person I needed to interact with, without knowing ahead of time that I needed to interact with them, and this was one of those times. I was experiencing the phenomenon of a person showing up in my life exactly as I needed them to, when I needed them to.

It was the beginning of a year of coincidence – or higher power intervention. As we spoke about what she had learned at the conference, I discovered that the field of psychiatry was opening up to a whole new concept of borderline… borderline as a *neurological* disorder, not just an Axis II personality disorder. A neurological disorder… like autism…

A light went on.

There is a plethora of brain studies on borderline personality disorder, much of it accessible via the internet. These studies support the biological etiology of this disorder – although it is widely known that chronic stress and trauma can change brain chemistry over time. The question then would be: Do the perceived traumas over time affect the physiology of the brain, or does the physiology of the brain create the perceived threats?

Over the past decade, research on the brain functioning of borderline patients has concluded that there are significant physiological components underlying the behavior and symptoms present in the disorder. Current thought leans toward borderline personality disorder as a neurobiological illness. MRI research has revealed that the part of the brain that processes and interprets threats, the hippocampus, is underdeveloped in a borderline patient. (Nasrallah 2014).

In addition, borderlines have a smaller, more active amygdala – the primitive part of the brain that processes fear.

Specifically, borderlines have increased amygdala response to facial expressions showing emotion - and some borderline patients had difficulty identifying neutral facial expressions, finding them threatening (Donegan 2003).

Meanwhile, as researchers at Weill Cornell Medical Center found in 2007, the prefrontal cortex was under-reactive in borderline patients. The prefrontal cortex is the more evolved part of the brain that processes emotions logically, and inhibits our primal urge to react. Brain studies have also shown decreased volume of gray matter in the anterior cingulate gyrus of borderlines, combined with reduced activity of the orbital frontal cortex – resulting in a regulatory system that fails to restrict expressions of emotion (New 2008).

So, it's the perfect storm: the brain of the borderline may be hardwired to overreact to neutral facial expressions, misperceive threats and alert the borderline to react, all while the emotional regulator is unresponsive. Retaliatory outbursts follow, whether self-injurious or externally aimed. The unrestricted emotional regulator, in turn, results in pervasive affective dysregulation, abandonment fears, and subsequent interpersonal impairments.

Further solidifying my resistance to the term borderline personality disorder: This may not be a true "personality disorder." It may be more of a neurological disorder than a personality flaw….like autism – and that, I understand.

My brother couldn't help it.

More light bulbs started to go on...

I've got this, David. I'm getting there.

Tweedle Dee and Tweedle Dum

> *"Curiouser and curiouser!" cried Alice*
> *(she was so much surprised, that for the moment*
> *she quite forgot how to speak good English).*

Lewis Carroll, Alice's Adventures in Wonderland -Chapter 2

Watching others struggle with a borderline loved one is very difficult. You either get sucked into the drama, or you develop a callousness to shield yourself against the Madness. For whatever reason, I've experienced borderline personality disorder close up more times than most people will. For the most part, I chose the shield.

My friend's wife was a borderline. I remember trying to explain it to him, then trying to find him a good counselor who could quickly identify and respond to the disorder. That proved to be a challenge. She was repeatedly diagnosed with depression, and medicated accordingly, which didn't help.

I was getting good at spotting borderlines – but still had no idea what one could do for them… or with them. I still did not fully understand what the disorder was, beyond pathological selfishness. I saw a disordered personality. An emotional hijacker. A doomsday timebomb.

His wife raised one red flag after another. She was over-emotional at Christmas because she didn't get enough presents - or worse - the *right* presents. He couldn't read her mind, and this was apparently a devastating experience for her.

She posted strange things on Facebook, like calling her dog her "confidant." She was also very jealous of his friends to the point of trying to isolate him from them.

The first time she tried to kill herself was after my friend had been asking her to please help clean around the house. She wouldn't get the kids ready for school or make them breakfast or dinner. If she went grocery shopping she bought Doritos and cupcakes. She didn't want to eat dinner at home - she wanted to eat dinner out, every night. She spent weekends in bed pouting if there weren't any plans to do something fun.

And she refused to clean. Or, in retrospect, she couldn't clean, due to a disorganized mind.

One Saturday afternoon, while she was out shopping for impulse items, my friend cleaned the house. When she arrived home and saw what he had done, she immediately started crying and ran out the door. She drove down some dirt road and made some cuts on her wrist with a razor blade. Then, she wrapped her wrist in a towel and called a friend to report what she had done … and told the friend where she was.

So… not exactly trying to commit suicide.

It seems she was trying to show her husband how upsetting his actions were. *I'll...show...you;* the borderline mantra.

She "showed him" a few more times over the next few years, during which time she completely changed her persona, changed groups of friends, withdrew from activities with the kids, and dabbled in recreational prescription drug use. As he put it, she needed chaos, and he was not a reactionary type of person.

On a Sunday morning, almost one year to the day after my brother's suicide, I got a text from my friend: "Well, it's over now."

I texted back, a few minutes later, "What is?"

He replied, "She is gone."

"Gone where?" I started to text back.

28

Then I paused and erased it. I suddenly knew what he meant. "Dead or disappeared?" I finally texted, just to be sure, but I knew.

Again.

She had finally succeeded in killing herself. It's hard to say whether or not she really meant to die. Borderlines are reckless in their attempts to prove to others how bad they feel inside. She took a handful of pills. The note she left behind just said something to the effect of, "if you call the ambulance I'll never speak to you again." It seems she did not quite grasp the finality of suicide.

Sadly, my unemotional account of her story illustrates the other side of the borderline entanglement. Aside from the one suffering from the disorder, and the ones suffering because of the disorder, there are those observers who are just fed up with the drama... the friends and loved ones who are fed up with the toll it has taken on the people they care about, and the toll it will continue to take on the people they care about. The people who fundamentally, in their hearts, believe the survivors are better off now.

I know who those people were in my story; the ones who felt that my brother's suicide was a mixed blessing. It doesn't mean they didn't care.

It actually meant they did care - and had cared all along – but they were at capacity.

Not all borderlines are suicidal and not all experiences with borderlines involve dealing with suicide attempts. The hallmark of the disorder is emotional dysregulation in response to misperceived threats. This is what dating a non-suicidal borderline male can look like:

- jealous rages over imagined infidelities (i.e. a friendly waiter)
- disappearing acts and behavioral retaliation in response to perceived "withholding"(i.e. the partner missed a phone call or made plans with a friend)

- infidelity – setting up lifeboats due to intense fear of abandonment (but then falsely accusing the partner of doing the same)
- borderline rages (you name it – one never knows when one will step on an eggshell around a borderline)
- incarceration – for aggression against someone who was a perceived threat (borderlines are often institutionalized)
- and, during moments of lucidity, acknowledgement that he had over-reacted (but always because the partner's behavior made him that angry, so technically it was the partner's fault)

So, why would anyone date a borderline? Well, for starters, no one starts out by telling you they are a borderline. They probably do not recognize that they are. And, of course, there are varying degrees of dysfunctionality within any disorder – so there's that. When not perceiving threat, borderlines can be their authentic, best selves. In the honeymoon stage of a relationship, they can present the best of who they are – and that can be pretty great. Unfortunately, humans are not perfect, and will invariably (unintentionally) hurt or disappoint one another. This is unacceptable for a borderline.

Functional borderlines are able to make a living, although they may change jobs frequently. They likely have a history of tumultuous relationships, but can be charismatic and fun to be around. They can be completely adoring at the beginning of a relationship, while the partner is still perceived as an unflawed person of light and thereby worthy of adoration… but the minute the partner becomes dark, (who knows why? Turned left instead of right? Took a phone call? Couldn't read minds?), the borderline can become a monster. A paranoid, spiteful, "I'll show you!" monster.

Sadly, "borderline" will always rear its ugly head, eventually – and the darkness, once set loose, envelops everything around it.

When I was out with Kelly one night, I remember remarking that it was statistically *impossible* that I would be surrounded by so many borderlines.

Kelly said, "No - it's obviously not statistically impossible… it is just statistically *unlikely*."

That phrase has resonated in my mind ever since, as my journey past my brother's suicide became curiouser and curiouser.

I had a lot of resentment for my brother in the decades before his death. I thought I knew what the disorder was, but I didn't give him a pass for being mentally ill. I knew that my friends and colleagues did not want to treat borderlines.
I knew that my friends who were struggling with borderline loved-ones were at the end of their ropes.
I saw the damage the borderlines caused and that was enough for me.

I don't specialize in borderline disorder. I specialize in psychometric testing. My areas of expertise are Autism, and most recently, Alzheimer's. For most of my career, I have done neuropsychological testing to diagnose disorders... I don't treat disorders. I don't know how to treat a borderline... and I wasn't my brother's therapist, so I wasn't even thinking about treatment. Unfortunately, I wasn't thinking about compassion, either. I was too angry.

He put my parents through hell. He stopped speaking to them for 10 years and only reached out after his wife left him. And in the 10 years that followed he talked to my dad for 3 hours a day on the phone – and during the calls ranged from lucid to self-deprecating to enraged. He tried to kill himself multiple times but always advertised it and called out for help. I saw it as emotional hijacking.

In the year following my brother's death I have delved into learning about the disorder. I have a new understanding of borderline personality disorder, and I want to get the message out: They can't help it. They can't help it because they can't see that their psychologically triggered perceptions are off. It is not simply pathological selfishness. It doesn't respond to medication, and illegal drug use *will make it worse.*

It is a neurological disorder that has to do with the function of brain, and in retrospect, I can attest that my brother was hard wired that way his whole life. Life events can trigger someone predisposed to borderline to be downright crazy… but some people live with the disorder, actively understanding that they need to look at their false perceptions and reframe.

I know that for many people, my brother's legacy is anger – and I want it not to be. I want the anger to be the legacy of the *disorder*, not the legacy of that poor, kind, sensitive soul who was engulfed by it.

My brother was a borderline. He killed himself - finally. And when that happened…. at that moment … all of the negative feelings I had toward him washed away, and all that remained was compassion. The darkness fell away, and all that was left was my little brother. And that's where my journey began.

In the year following his death, I have developed a compassion that I wasn't able to have when he was alive.

Do I wish I could have done things differently?
Yes, every day.

Could I have done anything differently?
At the time, no.

The "me" and the "him"
interacted exactly,
and only,
as we were able to.

And that's the only answer.

****

I didn't treat my brother as if he was made of glass.

I didn't believe he was made of glass – to me, he was just pathologically selfish.

But maybe he was made of glass.

****

Chapter Three
The Mad Hatter

"Who are you?" said the Caterpillar.
This was not an encouraging opening for a conversation.
Alice replied, rather shyly,
"I—I hardly know, Sir, just at present—at least I know who
I was when I got up this morning, but I think I must have been
changed several times since then."
"What do you mean by that?" said the Caterpillar, sternly.
"Explain yourself!"
"I can't explain myself, I'm afraid, Sir," said Alice,
"because I am not myself, you see." ―

Lewis Carroll, Advice from a Caterpillar – Chapter 5

My brother wore a white sox baseball cap and glasses. That's how people will remember him – his signature look posted all over his Facebook memorial page. The box bearing his ashes features a photo of him wearing his hat and glasses, on his last day in Chicago. Over the years, I remember that his glasses were always in some state of taped-up repair.

So now we hit the crossroad. Where do I go from here? Do I tell the real truth or do I edit... What is the right call?

His story is not my story to write. For that matter, my parents' story isn't my story to write. It's really just my story that is mine to share.

And what is that? My perception?

Here is my perception of the story:

I loved my little brother very much. His name was David.

David was a sensitive child. Oversensitive. Funny and talented, but quick on the trigger if he was angry. I remember that if my mom was separated from him in a store, he would become entirely too distressed. Back in the 70s, in a small town especially, our parents didn't keep us on a leash. We weren't always in sight of our parents, and that was normal, back then. As a child, I was allowed to look at things in a store and find my mother when I was done. Not David. He would look at things and if my mom moved on to another aisle, it was the end of the world for him. On more than one occasion, I remember him being so upset and angry about her being out of sight that his lips were actually blue by the time he found her, minutes later.

David and I did everything together: family vacations, camping, roller coasters, playing with Star Wars figures, making up silly stories…. I went to all of his all-star little league games and cheered him on until I lost my voice. We swam in the summer and snowmobiled in the winter.

We also fought - frequently. Sibling rivalry – nothing that I didn't see my friends experience as well. If I hit him, however, as young siblings do, or land a perfect verbal shot, I would have to run to my room and lock my door. He would go crazy and bang on the door, trying to break it down, until our mom intervened. Trying to wait it out was futile, though. Even after I thought the storm had passed, it hadn't. At some later time, out of the blue, I would get smacked in retaliation. That could occur hours or days later, but it would occur.

He retaliated against every slight… real or perceived. In retrospect, it makes sense. At the time, it was just David.

I have one very poignant memory, however, that sticks in my mind as a moment when a switch was flipped. It was indiscernible to everyone else in the room, but it has haunted me ever since. I was in high school – a senior, so he must have been a freshman. I had several friends over and we were all swimming. One of my male friends had learned of an incident where David had hit my leg with a fireplace poker, because I had made him mad a few days prior. I'm sure the original fight was mutual. I'm sure I did make him mad. I'm sure I was mad, too. At any rate, the guy felt the age-appropriate need to set him straight, male to male. He went up to David in the pool and said something to the effect that it wasn't ok to hit girls, even if she is your sister – and added that if it happened again, he would have to deal with him.

I remember cringing internally at the time. It was both age-appropriate, and culturally appropriate, for a teenage male to address that… but I knew, even as a teenager, that it was going to hit David hard. David got out of the pool and went into his room. Later we were all in the house watching TV, and David came out of his room wearing sunglasses. He looked like a Blues Brother, so everyone laughed. I even laughed…. until suddenly I realized that he was wearing the sunglasses because he had been crying. He didn't want us to see his red eyes. And that laughter was like a knockout punch to someone who had not been ready to get back up in the ring.

Normal boys would have shaken all of that off. Normal conventions told me that it was ok; that he would be ok.

In my heart I knew he wasn't normal, though.

My brain had not registered that yet, however, and wouldn't for a few more years.

Maybe, if I had started actually reading the textbooks that were collecting on my shelf – maybe, if I had stumbled across an article by Gunderson that would have helped me identify what we were actually dealing with - I could have done or said something to repair the damage of that day.

But how do you uncrack an eggshell?

In the late 80s, when I was in college, David would come down to my apartment on weekends and hang out with my roommates and me. He always seemed to enjoy his time with us.

David's best friend was Dan. They spent a lot of time together in high school. I didn't know Dan very well – in retrospect, David had started keeping his life fairly compartmentalized. He didn't bring friends around family.

I know that David and Dan had a lot in common: a love of the arts, a love of music … and a love of altered states of consciousness.

The field of transpersonal psychology – the field of psychology that recognizes the spirit as an integral component of the human experience – found its origins in the altered states of consciousness studies in the 1960s. Timothy Leary and Richard Alpert are widely credited with beginning practice in the field of Transpersonal counseling with their use of psychedelic drugs in their studies at Harvard University – for which they were subsequently fired. Transpersonal counseling considers altered states of consciousness - or peak experiences, as Abraham Maslow called them - to be both healing and transformative (Scotton 1996). The transcendent spiritual experiences during altered states of consciousness linked transpersonal psychology to biological practices of psychiatry – the belief that human psychopathology stems from the biological malfunction of the nervous system. (Scotton, 1996).

My brother's descent into Madness seemed to coincide with an increased use of illegal drugs when he went to college. While he bonded with friends during altered states of consciousness, and likely found significant artistic inspiration there as well, my guess is that the drugs also triggered the exacerbation of an existing biological malfunction in his brain. From all accounts, his musical artistic genius began to flourish during this time - but functionally and behaviorally, he began to decompose. It is likely that drugs and alcohol further damaged his already impaired frontal cortex, making him less reasonable and more susceptible and reactive to perceived threat.

I didn't see much of David after my junior year in college. At one point, he moved in with my boyfriend, Chris, and my friend, Brian. I graduated, got a job at a hospital, and started graduate school. I remember seeing my brother a few times on holidays. David was actively involved with his band, but I was never invited to a performance.

David's first suicide attempt occurred when he was in college. He apparently left a suicide note, which accompanied an intentional overdose of pills. A roommate called 911 and David reportedly became aggressive with the orderlies who came to take him away. "Thugs" he called them. Apparently, his struggle resulted in his glasses being broken, and him being strapped to a bed.

My mother asked me to go with her to see him at the inpatient facility. I had not seen David in a while, and when we were escorted to a prison-like holding room, I wasn't prepared for what my brother had been reduced to. He was sitting slouched over in a metal chair, dressed in hospital garb. His glasses were broken in the middle and precariously propped on his cheekbones. He had bruises on his face. His eyes were swollen and red.

There was nothing therapeutic about this place.

David looked up at me with an expression I'd never seen before: vacant and pleading at the same time. He begged me to get him out of there. He told me that they beat him up and strapped him to a dirty mattress that smelled like urine.

Then he said something that has impacted me throughout my professional career: "If I didn't want to kill myself before, I sure as hell do, now."

He felt demeaned, devalued and demoralized. Nothing good was going to come out of this….

The doctor came in, and with a heavy accent, proceeded to ask David if he knew why he was there. He told David, "You are here because you did something bad."

I will never forget that. I will never forget my feelings of shock and anger, or the look of humiliation on my brother's face. I felt his

38

sadness, his emptiness. He looked at the doctor and said, "My sister is a psychologist. Can't she sign me out of here?"

The doctor looked at me and said, "You're a psychologist?"

Actually, I was just an intern with the county school system. I still had no comprehension of what was going on with David, even though I could tell it was out of my depth, professionally. All I knew was that my brother was in a horrible place, and he was asking me to help him … so I did.

Sometimes, when someone asks you if you're a psychologist, you just say, yes.

And without even asking for my credentials, the doctor just signed David out to my care. He just let him go home with me. It clearly wasn't a therapeutic environment, and I really felt like taking my brother out of there was the right thing to do at the time – so I went along with it. My little brother was in pain and he was asking me to help him. He was afraid. He was in a terrible place, emotionally and physically, and people were being mean to him. I could not allow that. I fix things, and he believed I could fix this, too.

On the way home, David tried to light up a cigarette in the car. My mother asked him not to, and he started cursing at her. When I jumped in and backed up her request, telling him we would be home in a minute, David flew into a rage. He opened the car door and tried to jump out of the moving vehicle. So much for gratitude. So much for a return to normalcy. It didn't matter what I had done to help him, all that mattered was what I did to slight him.

I didn't see him again for a year, after that.

I didn't realize how dark he had become until his next birthday. That was the incident where he lashed out at me, out of the blue, for "treating him like shit his whole life." I didn't realize at the time that he was a borderline, of course, or how serious he was. I thought he was crazy, but didn't realize how crazy. At the time, I couldn't identify the allegation of abuse that was central to the borderline experience.

We were all at my parent's house that night. I brought my new boyfriend, and he brought his new girlfriend and his friend. My boyfriend was someone who was apparently repellant in every way to David, who had now become a long-haired, brooding, tortured artist-type. And unbeknownst to me, David had found an audience to enable his fantasies of having been abused and neglected as a child. After he started dating her, everything really went downhill for us as a family.

It's hard to blame someone for believing a loved one who claims to have been abused. He certainly acted like an abuse victim: low self-esteem (self-loathing, actually), fear of abandonment or hurt, overly sensitive to reactions of others. He only wore second hand Goodwill clothing, at that time. Of course, I didn't realize that, so I had purchased him a nice sweater for his birthday, because he was planning to move to Chicago. The polo emblem really set him off. I just remember thinking: What the heck is wrong with him???

There's nothing inherently dysfunctional about my family. At least I know that I didn't grow up in a dysfunctional family - and he had better parents than I did! Everything he did was wonderful. We went to all of his ball games, local and out of town. David didn't want them to come watch his high school play, but my Dad went anyhow. He sat in the back and didn't make a big deal of it, but he cared enough to go.

It seemed like if David drew anything on a piece of paper, it was framed and put on the wall…. My father took David to the guitar store every chance he got, and supported his music and sound engineering career… So, it didn't quite make sense that David believed he was abused or neglected or didn't get enough attention. Apparently, though, he just didn't get the kind of attention he wanted - whatever that was. Maybe he didn't get it from the world, maybe just from us – who knows.

At any rate, it got to the point where we were just walking on eggshells all the time around him as he entered early adulthood. Actually, "eggshells" is an understatement – it was more like a mine field. After 10 years of trying to avoid landmines, I'd had enough. He and his wife (the enabler) were visiting for Christmas. I was holding my toddler and pregnant with my second child, and I was talking to my mother about something that had nothing to do with him - and all the while he was pacing. Glaring at me, muttering and pacing. He had been drinking – and had probably finished off most of a bottle of vodka.

All of a sudden, I said something he didn't like during the conversation with my mother – and crack. An eggshell broke. He started ranting and cursing at me, like a crazy person. This time, however, something inside of me just snapped, as well – and I launched a verbal counteroffensive of biblical proportions.

He didn't speak to my me or my parents for 10 years after that. He'll show me…

The darkness is contagious. It sucked me in, too. It's almost like the Madness is an entity unto itself opposite of the spirit, and it battles the spirit for control of the body. It battles the soul. It's a dimensional existence that we don't understand… so we call it mental illness and treat it with drugs. But the darkness does not respond to medication. It responds to light.

David reached back out to my parents after his wife finally left him. I wasn't a fan of hers, but I'm sure he was a nightmare to live with. I blamed her for the chasm between my brother and my parents, but in reality, she was just occupying the passenger seat. The drugs derailed him; the enabling just kept him off course. She, at some point, must have gone dark to him, and then it would have been all downhill from there…

By the time he was back in touch with us, David needed a significant amount of help from my parents. His wife filed for divorce while he was hospitalized, so my father hired an attorney to make sure my brother's rights were not being violated. I know he was in a mental ward – I'm not sure of the details of that time in his life, though, since he hadn't been speaking to us. I do know that he attempted suicide at least 5 more times after that.

I was able to see a few of his public Facebook rants after his divorce. They were dark – too dark to reproduce here. I don't believe his soul still feels the horrible things that the darkness wrote about. Posts about hatred and violence. They were disgusting – but mostly the product of drunken borderline rage.   There was a point several years ago when I was sure that the feds would come get him – I'm sure his rants made him a crazy person of interest.

I believe the posts were mostly just for show, and because the people who loved him knew that, they kept loving him. The posts are gone now, as they should be. He was a borderline drowning in his worst fear: abandonment. Two classic non-clinical books about borderlines are *I Hate You, Don't Leave Me* (Straus and Kreisman 1991) and *Stop Walking on Eggshells* (Mason and Kreger 2010). The titles say it all. Driving loved ones away, then raging and panicking because they left – but constantly walking on eggshells is exhausting, and the borderline rage is abusive – no one should be expected to endure that – from either side of it.

Over the years, my dad kept a spreadsheet of David's diagnoses. He was diagnosed with almost everything at one point or another: major depressive disorder, bipolar disorder, post-traumatic stress disorder (*WTF??*), and autism (REALLY, *WTF?*).

All I knew was that he was being routinely misdiagnosed by Medicaid doctors. By that time, I knew he was a borderline.

The diagnoses given to my brother seemed like a joke - a blow off. It was like they just put down anything just to get paid on it, taking advantage of the Medicaid patient. I can't stand that. Kelly and I quit a job over that once… darn ethics always getting in our way.

The diagnosis that my brother was given that made me the most angry was "autism." He was not autistic as a child. I have a child on the autism spectrum. I have written a dissertation on autism. I know autism when I see it - David was not autistic.

At the height of his dysfunction he had an autistic presentation, because of his avoidance of eye contact, perseveration, over-focusing on things that weren't relevant to the rest of us, and emotional dysregulation - but this was not a case of adult-onset autism (which doesn't exist). My guess is that the avoidance of eye contact was rooted in shame and self-loathing. Perseveration was likely a result of increasing frontal lobe damage.

The other diagnosis that bothered me was PTSD. What was his trauma? No one could ever answer that for me.

My psychiatrist friend at work says that they treat the Axis 1 symptoms first. They try to address chemical imbalances in an effort to diminish the symptoms before they can get to the root of the personality disorder. That makes sense. My brother was on a cocktail of psychotropic meds. Uppers in the morning, downers in the afternoon.

My father said that in the final months in Chicago, David did find someone who seemed to know exactly what he was dealing with, and tried to wean David off of the medication and into therapy. Apparently, David raged against that. I remember him on the phone calling that therapist every name in the book. David believed he needed his drugs, and no one was going to take them away from him. He also lacked insight, and seemed to like it that way.

David's multiple suicide attempts were not terribly lethal, by design, and were always preceded with a warning shot and accompanied by fanfare. He took pills and left a note; he slit his wrists live on skype; he brought his grill inside and lit it up – but he let his dogs out to run and bark the courtyard. The neighbors heard the dogs bark and saw the smoke– and pulled him out of the gas fumes. Every attempt seemed to be designed to be both punctuating and preventable – if someone was paying attention.

And someone always was.

When his ex-wife found out that he had attempted suicide again, during a week that he had "dog visitation" (that's an entirely different discussion), she decided to defy the court order and refuse to send the dogs back to him again.

The dogs were David's whole world. Losing them was a fatal crack in what was left of the fragile protective shell around him.

Only dogs can give enough attention to a borderline to consistently fill the void, inside. Without his dogs – it is likely that the chronic emptiness he felt was unbearable.

So, the non-lethal suicidal behaviors continued. Benign bullshit attempts, as I had begun to call them in my head: the signature move of the borderline. From the outside, it just looks and feels like emotional terrorism. Borderlines emotionally hijack those who love them and keep them on the hook - because one false move, one cracked eggshell, and they'll try to kill themselves. And their loved ones are well aware of that. "I'll show you - just watch."

I didn't react to him with much compassion in the end. He brought out the worst in me. The darkness envelops all around it. It's contagious. I would try to avoid negative interactions, but there was nothing in him for me to connect with anymore. At least not that I could see.

David would say antagonistic things just to bait me in to a fight… or maybe just to show me how awful he was, to confirm it for himself…
In retrospect, it was probably the latter.

What was going on inside of him had to have been horrific. Perception of hostility in others, paranoia, intense fear of being alone yet an inability to stop himself from striking out at driving people away. Unendurable emptiness. My dad says that in the end, David knew exactly what he was, and he hated it. He talked to my dad for 3 hours a day on the phone, and lived with my parents, for his final month on earth. David knew he would wake up and take the first round of his daily prescription cocktail, uppers, and be OK for a little while; then slowly start descending into the pit.

It must have been hell.

David would take prescription downers in the afternoon to sedate himself. *One pill makes you larger…. And one pill makes you small… And the ones that mother gives you, don't do anything, at all…go ask Alice, when she's ten feet tall*[1]. My parents did not know about the drugs and alcohol he was also taking daily on the side to self-medicate, but Alice knew. And my parents will know now, too, when they read this.

David reached out to me toward the end, just before he moved here. It was surprising to me at the time – hopeful. He messaged me a clip of a children's show we watched as kids in Canada. He said he stumbled on it and it made him laugh. I messaged back that I was planning to take the kids on a road trip from Florida to Western New York and Canada, to see the towns where we grew up. Everything seemed fine, and then the messages stopped.

A few hours later I got a text from the pit: "If you see any of my old friends, please tell them I'm dead… not far from the truth, anyways."

That was May 27, 2017. I did not respond. A month later, after he died, I looked back at that rare handful of messages I had exchanged with him and was struck by the fact that I just hadn't responded. How does one respond to that, though? I remember wondering at the time if I should respond, or if it was just kindling waiting for me to say something unintentionally incendiary. I suppose I was just taking a moment before responding… and then life happened, and time moved on.

I ended up not taking the kids to Canada due to a weather front, and instead we found ourselves on route to Alaska the very next day. That trip had been my biggest accomplishment, to date.

We spent a week on an Alaskan Disney cruise… with no cellular service and no internet. I contacted no one. By the time we got back home, David was in the process of moving to Florida, and I had forgotten all about the strange message.

Did it bother him that I never responded to his message of death? I have no idea. I never had the chance to ask about it. My guess is that he was in the middle of a downward spiral into darkness when he sent the message, probably drinking, probably lashing out on multiple venues, to multiple audiences. He may not have even remembered the text.

I did not want David to move back here. I railed against it. I thought of him as a doomsday timebomb and knew he would wreak havoc on the family. I was right, but I take no satisfaction in that. To my parents, he was their child. They loved him. He was welcome back home. He always had been.

I live a few blocks from my parents. My sons, especially my youngest, spend a lot of time over there. I worried about exposing them to someone that I knew as unstable… and borderline rage can be dangerous.

My mom made dinner at night, and the boys and I would often go over for family meals. David and I didn't interact. He made statements to the room, but never anything directed toward me or inviting of conversation. I would make casual dinner conversation and he would just glaze over and not participate.

One night, it hit me that he seemed completely void of an ability to have a normal give-and-take conversation. Most of what he talked about was self-centered and myopic. He seemed to be limited to talking about his own experience. His social interaction skills were shockingly impaired.

This was the child who was voted student council president in middle school, just before we left Canada. He was the celebrated first basemen for the all-star little league team, year after year. He was the performer who played in bands and recorded music for struggling artists.

I did not know much about David, professionally, but I did know that he was widely acknowledged as a sound engineering genius, whose business ideology was that quality song recording should be accessible to all. He launched the initial recording efforts for many musicians over the years, sometimes taking trades instead of cash. So how did he get to this dysfunctional place, so bereft of skills of social interaction?

He would talk about something he was interested in and if one of us tried to respond, he would glaze over - and then after we were done talking, he would go right back to where he left off, as if no one had spoken.

I remember being caught off guard one night at dinner when he asked how everyone's steak was. It was kind of a blanket question to the table. He asked it earnestly, sounded interested in our experience - which surprised me – until I realized that the question was about him. *He made the ste*aks. He didn't ask if we enjoyed our day, seen any good movies lately, or anything else about what we were experiencing. He never did.

He asked if we like the steaks because he had made the steaks. He didn't ask if we had liked the macaroni salad that my mother had made. He didn't ask if anyone liked the wine I brought. He didn't ask how the kids were doing in school. His questions were always related to his experience. He had lost his empathy.

But, who am I to judge? I had lost empathy, too.

One of the last vivid memories I have of David's final days was when we were all sitting down for dinner at my mother's house and his phone rang. David became very excited because it was a call from his friend, Ray. David thought the world of Ray and his brother, 'Mando. He answered the phone at the table, loudly exclaiming, "Ray!", and proceeded to talk loudly and excitedly in front of all of us… still at the dinner table... I remember feeling annoyed that he needed so much attention. There was an uncomfortable sense that he was trying to show us he had a friend.

How sad that would be, to feel like you have to prove you have a friend. I should have felt sad - for him. But at the time, I was depleted. Annoyed. Exhausted and exasperated. He was taking too much attention and energy, already. Apparently, my mother was depleted too, because she suggested he take the call outside. He went outside - just on the other side of the sliding glass door, and continued to speak loudly so that we could hear everything he said.

Now I realize that it was probably not about us, at all. It's likely that he spoke loudly because he was in his own experience, oblivious to our experience.

He and I had very little interaction after he moved back, and when we did, it went south, quickly. He wouldn't have had it any other way. The last time I spoke to him was a few weeks before he died. It was just before Father's Day. I was at my parents' house after work one night. Mom and I were drinking wine. David was sitting in the kitchen nearby and my son, Quentin, was next to me on the couch. I asked my mother what we were doing for Father's Day dinner. She said, "David is planning to make dinner."

David spoke up. "Not anymore," he muttered.

"Why?" mom asked. This wasn't going anywhere good, I could just tell.

"Because Quentin is a fucking asshole." David snapped.

Ok, I'm in, now… no staying out of this…

Quentin was 15 at the time - a loving, 15-year-old boy, on the autism spectrum, who had a passion for cooking. Quentin is a very kind soul. He only sees hearts – he responds to the light in people, and doesn't react negatively to darkness. He seems to find the darkness to be ironic.

When his paternal great-grandmother with dementia told him that she 'hopes he drowns', he just laughed and said, "No you don't, Gramma Jane." He hears her words, and loves her, anyhow. Her nasty comments are ironic to him, because he sees her heart. He never knew her before her mind went, but I did – and I liked her, too.

So, when David said what he did, it did not bother Quentin the way it bothered me. He just looked up and laughed in surprise. "What did I do?" he said.

Apparently, David had previously told him that he was going to make his specialty dish involving chicken, broccoli, rice and Worcestershire sauce. Quentin, being a chef, simply asked: *Why Worcestershire instead of soy sauce?* It was a normal question, and very typical of Quentin, who liked to understand things and learn. David cursed and sputtered out the story, as if he was egregiously and intentionally slighted by this child. A child who was really only interested in how the dish might taste, and how it might be different from, or better than, a way he had previously experienced it. David was now refusing to make dinner – and he made that very clear. With expletives.

Quentin was unphased.
I took another sip of wine. Déjà vu. This wasn't going anywhere good… and it was going there fast.

I said, "Ok then Quentin can make Father's Day dinner," and I took another sip of wine. Done with this.

My mother, who was happy to have the subject diverted, said, "That's a good idea," and then the fatal question, "Quentin, what are you going to make?"

Poor Quentin. He said the only thing he would say: "I think I'd like to make chicken, broccoli, rice and Worcestershire sauce."

Click. Landmine.

David went off - calling my son a "fucking asshole" over and over.

I remained seated but put my wine down. I said, very calmly, "David, you will not curse at my children and you will not call them names."

David said, "Fuck you. What are you going to do about it?"

I looked him straight in the eye, and without raising my voice – which was quite atypical for me – said, "I will say this one more time. You will not curse at my children, and you will not call them names. Is that clear?"

And David looked me square in the eyes right back, darkness inking out like smoke around him and said, "What are you going to do about it?"

I saw the darkness permeating the room. It took hold of me, too. I stood up, and I took the fatal shot that only a sibling could take. I laughed at him.

"What am I going to do about it?" I replied. "What would I even need to do, David? What more could I do to you that you haven't already done to yourself?" Darkness curling up like smoke around my words.

I said what I needed to say to shut that crazy train down. I didn't want to mortally wound him, I just wanted him to stop. I did not want to be among mad people, or to be one of them.
The darkness is contagious, and it had always sucked me in, in the past... and this time, I just wanted out.

That was the last time I ever saw my brother. He was dead a few weeks later.

I left my parents' house and took my boys with me. They were not allowed to go back to their grandparents' house while David was there. I just didn't think it was an appropriate situation for them. Since I was the only person who would stand up to David or call out his inappropriate behavior, and I sure as heck wasn't going back there, I didn't think they were safe. I have a license, a life, a career-there was no way I was going to endanger any of that to engage with a borderline.

Sometimes, it seemed that David just tried to be awful. And he was awful. He was hard to be around. *What more could I do to you that you haven't done to yourself?* I couldn't take it back, and didn't try.

I didn't know he was going to be dead soon. I didn't want him to be. I wanted him to be alive, but not acting like a dark crazy person anymore. How could we ever function as a family if someone didn't identify boundaries – hard limits, like don't curse at my autistic child…. There was nothing not awful about any of it.

My little brother used to be kind and lovable and funny and brilliant and talented. This disorder took everything from him, and from us. It took all of the could- and should-have-beens, a long time ago, and that's why this book is being written.

My brother was a kind, sensitive soul who became engulfed by the darkness of borderline personality disorder.

I wish it could say that my brother was wonderful and that I miss him. In the last half of his life, however, my brother was angry and hostile toward me, my parents, and several friends who had been blown off the path by borderline rage. He was Anakin Skywalker as a child, and then the darkness consumed him. It's as simple, and as complicated, as that. I could no longer see the wonderful, he wouldn't let me… but I can say, honestly, for the first time in 20 years, I do miss him.

There are several people who also miss him very much. Thankfully, there are people for whom David was wonderful, right until the end - his friend Ray being one of them. Ray, apparently, never went dark, and he was able to see my brother's authentic self. He was a Ray of light in David's eyes. And through my family's darkest hour, he was a ray of light for us, too.

****

Mom's Facebook post. August 2017

60 days ago, David watched as all of his worldly possessions, including all of his instruments and equipment for his recording studio, were loaded onto a moving van.

Two weeks later when the van arrived at our front door, David's belongings were not on the truck. David was devastated. At first, we were told they had no idea where his load was. You all know what happened after that.

His dad made daily phone calls and emails to the moving company who assured us this was a "priority." Finally, about two weeks ago, we were told they had located his things and would be loading soon. Last night we got a call from the truck driver that the equipment was loaded, and he was leaving Chicago. We spoke about descriptions of things on the load, and it looks like it is actually David's things. The load should be here tonight or tomorrow morning.

Good news, but I am already crying as I think about watching his prized possessions being unloaded and how much it would have meant to David if they had been delivered as promised.

****

When David's stuff went missing, we were all very upset. A moving van finally did arrive at my parents' house – several days later than expected – but as they started unloading, David realized that it wasn't his stuff. They did not have his things on the van, and everything he owned, including his guitars and sound engineering equipment, had vanished without a trace. His whole life was unaccounted for. I was not there at the time, but I'm sure it was an understandably heated scene. I cannot imagine what that would feel like, to have everything of value to you disappear into thin air. It would push a normally functioning person over the edge.

From all accounts, David had been very hopeful about moving back to Florida. It was time to leave Chicago. The landlord was selling his condo, and he had exhausted his resources there. More specifically, he was burning bridges. Apparently, following separate incidences, both David's ex-wife and his former bandmate, Brian, had each called Dan, asking him to get in touch with David's parents. David was disintegrating. He was going off the rails.

When I was an intern, I worked with a woman named Joan. We had a lot in common, despite our difference in age. We met for dinners after work, and had wonderful, inspirational conversations. It took almost a full year for us to realize that my brother David and her son, Dan, were best friends.

She knew David very well – all through high school David had spent a great deal of time at her home. When David moved to Chicago, he lived with Dan, and when he stopped speaking to his family, Joan was still in contact with him, seeing him when she visited her son in Chicago.

Over the years, Joan became an integral part of our family. My boys call her Grammy. She comes to our house for all holidays, so her son Dan truly did have a direct connection to my parents, despite the fact that he had been blown off of David's path, many years ago, for whatever reasons.

It must have been very surreal for David when he first came home, after being gone and out of touch for over a decade. He re-emerged into a family he didn't know. He did not know my children, but here they were, two boys who were the apples of his parents' eyes.

There was a new true north on the family compass. It must have been very disorienting. And to top it off, "Mrs. K", as he still called her until the end, was now "Grammy Joan" to the rest of his family.

Joan loved David and he thought the world of her. He actually tried to interact with her. I noticed him soften when she was around. She was still light.

Initially, the moving company could not find David's belongings, and could not account for their whereabouts. After a few calls and emails, they stopped responding to my father, altogether. David already had a bad feeling about the moving company, before he left Chicago. He said they demanded more money after they loaded his things on the truck. He felt threatened, and called my father for help. Of course, borderlines often perceive threats where there is none – but in this case, when his treasured guitars and amplifiers and sound recording equipment went missing, we all assumed foul play.

It was a truly horrible feeling.

After a few weeks, David and my father got word that the truckload was found, and on its way down to Florida. Apparently, David's belongings had been taken to a holding facility, pending transport to Florida. The original guys who picked up David's things were just local contractors. The big cross-country trucks owned by the van lines hold more than one customer's belongings - so they wait until they have a full truckload heading to the same destination before they dispatch new drivers to transport the contents and deliver them to various addresses.

When they finally arrived at my parent's house and started unloading David's things, he realized they *weren't* his things.
My mother said he became very upset and started yelling. I would have lost my mind.

Two days later, my brother was gone, forever.

The day after the truck incident, my mother came to my house to help me paint my master bedroom. My dad and son, Aidan, were taking on my bedroom remodel project. My father was hoping to get David involved, as well, when he got back from his stay at the beach. David had made plans to go to Ormond beach for a week. Quentin says he helped him pick out the hotel.

My mother, Aidan and I were painting my walls, when David called. He was upset and wanted my mother to come home, but she was busy painting. He called a few times, like a child. I remember my mother trying to speak logically to him – explaining that she was in the middle of painting – covered in paint, actually - but would be home as soon as she got cleaned up. She was doing the cutting in, and Aidan was rolling paint on the walls. It went very quickly… on our end.

I'm sure it was like dog years on his end. His mother was withholding – one of the worst things a borderline thinks you can do.

Apparently, David and my father had been arguing. Quentin was actually there, at the time. After a few weeks of taking a stand, I had loosened up a bit and allowed my boys to go back over for short periods during the day. It was summer, they were out of school, and I worked all day. Quentin said they were yelling and David said mean things about Gramma and Grampa. He said Grampa told him that if he didn't want to live there, he could leave.

David never spoke to him again.

By the time David's friend picked him up the next morning, he was in full borderline rage mode. Between his missing stuff, his parents not jumping fast enough and his friend not answering the phone the night before, it was a trifecta. The perfect storm on a Monday morning. He asked my mother for money and told her he was going to see Ray in California.

Then, he looked at her with black eyes – she says she'll never forget how black his eyes were - and he said the last words he ever spoke to her: "You will never see me again."

She never did.

All we got back from the coroner were the hat and the glasses.

****

Dan's Facebook post – July 2017

hi everyone, i wrote this a couple of days ago... I was friends with dave during high school and through his mid twenties. and when dave started pushing his friends away, I was one of the people that got pushed. I write about 'moving on and hoping for the best'...

I would like to take this opportunity to thank those that never 'moved on' from dave...

I'm also including a couple of drawings dave created. I've held on to them for 30 ish years, and I think they are still cool.

dealing with a friend with a mental illness is like this: you want to help, yet they don't want your help. you want to care but they don't want you to care. you want to love them but they aren't interested. so you move on and hope for the best for them.

my best friend from high school killed himself this week after a long fight with mental illness. I mourn the loss of his life today, but i mourned the loss of my friend years ago…

****

Chapter Four
<u>**Off With Their Heads**</u>

"(Alice) had never forgotten that if you drink much
from a bottle marked 'poison'
it is almost certain to disagree with you sooner or later."

— *Lewis Carroll, Alice's Adventures in Wonderland - Chapter 1*

That Monday was the last day anyone saw or heard from David.
There was an outgoing message from him to Ray. His friend had
dropped him off at the hotel in Ormond beach where he had made
plans to stay a month prior, and then she went home. His friend later
said that David got angry with her for leaving. Of course he did. She
was "withholding" – the worst thing you can do to a borderline - and
he was a full-blown borderline, who had lost any ability for
acknowledging the perspective of someone who went dark. He
called Ray at some point Monday night. After that, radio silence.

He wouldn't answer the phone, so his friend went back to the hotel
the next day. She knew he was mad at her. She knocked on the door
and he wouldn't answer. He had not made any threats of suicide, as
he had every time in the past, so she had no reason to assume he was
in trouble. She assumed he was either out, or didn't want to speak to
her. Either scenario was feasible.

On Wednesday I was sitting at work. I looked up and said to
<u>Khakie,</u> "I think my brother is dead." Her eyes widened, a little.
I'm sure that the matter of fact presentation startled her.

I just had a strange sensation; *a disturbance as if a million voices*
cried out in terror and were suddenly silenced2...   I no longer felt

the darkness. I didn't find out for a year that my mother had a similar sensation that day.

Suicide is like a grenade. It takes everyone out around it. You can be personally traumatized by the suicide of someone you haven't thought of in years...

Many times, when people kill themselves, the survivors are left to question why. I have spoken with people who have lost loved ones to suicide and say that years go by and they still question, why.

As I said before, with a borderline, you don't really question why. Oftentimes, a borderline has made so many attempts that everyone just comes to an understanding that they were past their point of tolerance for suffering. Or that they're striking out, and they will sacrifice themselves just to "show you" how much you hurt them.

With a borderline, you don't question why - you question why you didn't react differently.

You question yourself ... but, then again, that was the intent of the act.

My grief experience is not unique. We are mortal, and we die - and as such, people around us die; people we love die; pets we love die. Grief is grief. The experience of trauma following a suicide, however, is a little different than the normal grief pattern. It's complicated grief.

The stages of grief are very generally defined as shock, anger, denial and sadness – then, various self-help sources will add in negotiating and questioning – ultimately leading to acceptance. You can move through the stages or you can bounce all around. You can start-over a hundred times before you get to acceptance. A suicide adds a trauma to the process. You've been hit by shrapnel from a terrorist.

Unlike other types of death, the deceased holds the identity of both victim and aggressor.

The illusion that they could have chosen differently haunts us.

A reality that they may have done this to strike out and hurt, tortures us.

My friend Brian said to me once, "When someone intentionally tries to hurt you emotionally, you can't blame yourself for feeling hurt, any more than you'd blame yourself for the pain if they had shot you with a gun." Borderline suicide attempts are often retaliatory. Some of David's past suicide attempts were fundamentally about striking out, and he was really angry with almost everyone on the day he overdosed.

When I called Quentin after work that Thursday, and he told me on the phone that my brother was dead, I cried all the way home. It was an hour and a half commute – blurred by tears and punctuated with guttural wails. All of my anger toward him fell away, and all that was left was grief over David, my little brother.

This is why my mother had chosen to wait to tell me - there was nothing I could do, an hour and a half away, and I still had my own patients to see that day, and a long commute home. The intention was not for me to find out at the beginning of the drive home, but Quentin was hurting and needed his mother. He needed to talk to me. He had suffered all day with his own sadness, and the pain of watching his grandparents grieve. He waited until I was done with work, and then he needed his mom. I just had to make it home, driving 70 mph through tears on the turnpike.

I stopped by my house to pick up my oldest son, Aidan, before heading to my parents' house. I stepped out of the car and suddenly felt the wind knocked out of me. This was not what I expected. I thought I had been prepared for this, all those years. I thought this would be different, more peaceful – but this was devastation. It took all of my strength to stand there in the garage, hands on my knees. Aidan heard the garage door and came out. He reached out to me and I hugged him. I hugged my boy and thanked God he was full of light.

That evening remains a blur of tears and regrets. I was just so sorry that I had fought with my brother. I was so sorry that I hadn't had the tools to deal with him. I was so sorry because I was constantly in a situation of having to defend against his hostility. He was no match for me and I knew it - but he got both barrels, anyhow.

On the third day after David passed my mother finally stopped crying and said, "I really feel like I've gotten through the hardest part. I feel like I've moved through the stages of grief and I've gotten through it and I'm just able to accept it now."

I said, "Well considering the fact you're in denial, I would say that's not accurate."

Poor Mom. She said, "I'm not in denial. I know he's dead. I just keep thinking, *I wish I would have done something*, or *what could I have said...* and of course I keep thinking about that - that's all I think about."

I said, "Mom. You are not even close to being through the stages of grief... and, honestly, I don't think you or Dad have any concept of the tidal wave that is about to hit you."

My mom still cries all the time. It's been a year.

For the first few days after David died, all my dad did was isolate facts and timelines. He and David talked for hours every day during his final years. My father had listened with unrelenting patience to David rant or complain or just comment on the banality of life.

After David passed, my father needed everything to be logical, and the facts led up to a simple conclusion: David knew what he was, and he hated what he was. That was David's mantra. He had told my father that, after one suicide attempt where he had to be revived, he remembers waking up in the hospital and feeling very upset that he was alive. He told Dad that he distinctly remembered that it felt so good *not* to be alive.

And my dad felt so much better when he was able to talk about those facts.

"You didn't have to do this, Dave." That's what my dad keeps saying. I would argue that he did have to do this. That was the progression of his disorder. I don't think there was a scenario in which he would have survived it...

Grammy Joan took it very hard, as well. She loved David and she loves my family. She went to dinner with us that Friday night, the night after we got the news. We had to eat. My kids needed some normalcy, and I needed a frozen chalice of beer from Tibby's. Joan has a sweet naivety about her, which belies her wisdom. She has also been struggling with deafness most of her life. That combination provided exactly the comic relief we needed that night. Misunderstood quips and innocent responses. We went from crying to laughing and back again at that dinner table. In her grief, she needed to be with us, as much as we needed to be with her.

Joan is terminally ill. Her memory is failing. She keeps saying that she hopes that I finish this book in time for her to read it.

Joan spent a lot of time with us those first few weeks. She told me she couldn't stand to be around anyone who wasn't us, right now, because no one else understands what she is going through - and she doesn't have the energy to even try to explain to them how she's feeling - or what she's feeling - or what this feels like - or what this is - or anything about this experience. No, she just wants to sit quietly with us.

I explained to her that it's not just grief, it's trauma. What she's experiencing is trauma. It's like when war veterans come home, and they seek out the company of other war veterans because no one else can possibly understand what they're experiencing. There's no way to put in words. Words minimize the experience. This is beyond words. This is sadness and horror and guilt - and it's just the beginning. It's devastation. No - there is no word that doesn't minimize it.

When people are sick and suffering, we wish them a quick, easy passing. We believe it will be a relief when they finally go. Suicide feels like the opposite of relief. Suicide launches the survivors into an abyss… and no one is ever relieved when their arm is blown off by a grenade. I thought it would be a relief. I was wrong. This is not relief – it is a chasm in my heart.

I told Joan that I didn't know how to write this book. I was having some strange experiences, and the story was going down a different path than I had anticipated. I wanted to write a clinical account, but my experience started becoming more and more spiritual - paranormal, even – so who would the audience even be?

Joan just smiled and said, "There was a time when it wouldn't have been the same audience - but it may actually be the same audience, now."

Joan has promised to live long enough to read this book.

I am writing as fast as I can.

● ●

We had a viewing for immediate family at the Funeral home, before
David was cremated. He had just moved back to Florida after 20
years in Chicago – we had no idea who he was still in contact with
here, or even how to reach them. The only people in attendance
were my parents, my two sons, and Joan. I'm pretty sure David
would have protested about us making even that big of a production.

I woke up the morning of the viewing and felt lost. Really lost. I
suddenly had no idea what to wear – and as the morning wore on, I
found myself just staring into my closet. It was such a simple thing,
but choosing an outfit was proving to be an insurmountable task for
me, in that moment. I didn't want to wear black; I knew that. I'd
had enough of the darkness, and now that we were out of it, I did not
want to go back.

Every day at work, my team and I coincidentally showed up wearing
outfits of the same color. There were three of us, at the time... and
we would all come to work in the same hues and tones as if we were
walking a runway in the same collection. Eggplant, Aquamarine,
Cerulean blue... People thought we called each other the night before
and planned it.

My coworkers were really there for me when I needed them. They
gave me space, but checked in periodically while I was out on
bereavement– and if I texted them, they texted right back. On the
morning of the viewing I found myself in a space of white noise. I
texted work: "The viewing is today and I don't know what to wear.
What color are we wearing?"

Joy responded immediately and without question. "Blue."

"Blue it is," I said.

According to my mother, my dad had been playing "Peace in the
Valley" on his guitar since the day they received word that David
had died. She kept saying he was going to take his guitar and play it
at the viewing.

My parents went to the funeral home ahead of us. Quentin rode with them. Aidan and Joan rode with me. When we were leaving the house, I asked Aidan if he wanted to bring his guitar - and he said he did. When we walked in the door of the funeral home, David's music was playing on sound system. It caught me off guard, hearing his voice. It was so strange – surreal. The woman at the desk showed us where the door was. My parents were already inside.

We walked through the doors into a large room with an open casket at the far end. My dad walked up to us and said, "He's cold." A fact, indeed. I knew what he was meant, though - if it had been my son in that casket, I would have been deeply affected by the same observation.

My boys didn't know how to respond. We all just stood there, at a notably awkward distance from the casket. My mom walked up to us and echoed my father: "He's cold." It struck me then that they had obviously touched him. Of course, they had. That dead body was poignantly still David to them. It was their son, and he was cold. He had been in the refrigerator. There could be no realization more chilling than that.

I have one true phobia and it's dead things. It's called necrophobia, and it's crippling. I would be fine with a live mouse in the house, but a dead one would shut me down. I could no more walk up to that casket with ease than someone with fear of heights could walk over and look out over a balcony. It took me a long time to get near the casket. I had a visceral reaction to it every time I looked toward it. My hands were sweating I was shaking. I could barely focus.
The last to do so, I finally walked over and forced myself to look at my brother's body. I stood there for a minute and then moved away as quickly as I could without making it obvious that I was having a difficult time. I was terrified that he was going to open his eyes and sit up, which is irrational on so many levels, because if my brother did come back to life it would have been a wonderful thing …but phobias are phobias. And it wasn't my brother. It was a casing without life. It was neither light nor dark. And one thing had been true about my brother in life: he was either very light, or very dark.

No, my brother wasn't in there.

I asked my mom if my dad was going to play guitar, but she said that last minute, he wouldn't bring his guitar. He told her he knew he would simply not be able to get through the song. At my request, Aidan went to the car to get his guitar and brought it back in to the room. I was aware that he didn't quite know what he should do, but he sat down in the back of the room, and I heard him quietly start to play "Dust in the Wind." It was beautiful. A teenage boy typically does not have a repertoire of funeral music. One song would have been enough, but my Aidan is a trooper. An Eagle Scout.

And when I heard him pick the first few bars of a soft, acoustic version of "Don't Fear the Reaper", I knew he was a warrior.

I looked up from the front of the room where the rest of us were quietly gathered and said, "Aidan, you rock."

My son had the guts to play a song about suicide at my brother's funeral. Ray had posted a video meme on Facebook, where David is cupping his hands on his mouth and shouting, "Play it with Balls!" Baton handed to you, my son.
It had been a week since David died, and Aidan hadn't cried. He just kept saying, "I didn't really know him."

I said, "You didn't know him that well, but you went with him and Grandpa to the guitar store for the past few years, when he came in town. You sat and jammed with him a few times. What do you mean you didn't know him?"

And he just said, "I didn't know him."

That's all he would say. His friends called him with condolences and his answer was always, "I didn't really know him." He was not going to allow himself to grieve. He was angry. His family had been devastated. His grandfather, who was the strongest man he'd ever known, was brought to tears every day. He didn't know what to do, so he steeled himself against everything and decided to be the rock for the family. He had allowed us to hug him, sobbing, at various points during the week, but he remained stoic. He *didn't know him*, he said. He held on to that.

I said to him at one point, "Aidan you did know him a little, but even if you feel like you didn't, your entire family is breaking down. That doesn't make you feel sad? It's okay to feel sad for other people."

And Aidan said, "No, it just makes me mad."

But Aidan is a quiet, gentle person, so his anger was quiet. He was strong. He stepped up when his grandfather couldn't, and pulled out his guitar and played in the funeral home. He played quietly, in the back, while the rest of us said goodbye.

As our time was winding down, I asked Aidan to move closer to the front of the room and play Dust in the Wind again, from beginning to end, as our final goodbye. We all sat down around him, and he started to play that familiar intro. All of a sudden, he started weeping – his head bent over the strings as he began crying harder, and harder, his body wracked with sobs.

My Dad walked over and gently took the guitar and the pic from him, and through teary eyes, he said, "Thank you Aidan. You just delivered the service."

Then my Dad sat down with the guitar and performed the song he had been practicing all week for my brother's funeral, "Peace in the Valley" – the one he didn't think he could find the strength to play.

And he got through the whole thing.

****

Mom's Facebook post:

David's official date of death was Thursday. However…on Wednesday evening I was overwhelmed by gut-wrenching emotion. I said to Paul, "David's in trouble, I think he gone."

We tried calling his cell phone for hours and left him numerous messages, begging him to call us.

I knew in my mother's heart he was gone and there was nothing I could do but cry. On Thursday morning it occurred to us to check my computer, and through his internet search history, we found the motel where he had made reservations. We called the motel. They rang his room with no answer. After several calls I told the clerk I was his mother and that I was very worried about him. She told me check out was at 11 am. The last time I called was about 11:15 and I asked the clerk if he had checked out. Her reply…………
"Oh, he's dead."

To add insult to injury, the clerk added, "Are you the same old lady who was calling about him earlier?"

****

Chapter Five
<u>Curiouser and Curiouser</u>

"Alice laughed: "There's no use trying," she said;
"one can't believe impossible things."

"I daresay you haven't had much practice," said the Queen.
"When I was younger, I always did it for half an hour a day.
Why, sometimes I've believed as many as six impossible things
before breakfast."

Lewis Carroll, Alice in Wonderland – Chapter 12

In the days following David's passing, my mother and I began
noticing that our eyeglasses were being moved from the places
where we normally kept them. My mother's reading glasses, which
were normally kept next to her computer went inexplicably missing.
After searching for them for quite some time, she finally found them
– on the table in the living room next to the chair where David used
to sit.

There was no explanation for why they would be there. She had
worn them a few times since he left, but only when she was sitting at
the computer in the kitchen. She had a few more experiences like
that with her glasses. She would reach out to get the pair of reading
glasses that were next to her bed, and find that they were simply not
there. Always, they would be found elsewhere, in a place she was
not likely to have left them.

Of course, I believed her. I have had paranormal experiences since I
was a child. A few days after David died, we went to dinner for
Aidan's birthday. Life has to go on. I drove, and we played David's
original songs, including his classic, "Everybody's Such and
Asshole." In playing his music, it felt as if we had invited David

along for the evening - and I'm sure he was with us. Actually, I know he was, because he took my glasses.

After dinner we came home. I sat upstairs, around my big dining room table, listening to my brother's recordings. I had never heard many of them before. Ray sent them to me on a USB drive.

I found myself crying uncontrollably. Why was it that I had never been given the opportunity to listen to his songs, before tonight? I was never able to tell my brother how much I enjoyed his music, because I had never heard it. I never had the chance to talk to him about his songs, and never experienced him laughing in my face at what he would have perceived as my lack of artistic taste.

I listened and mourned that I would never have a conversation with him about his music, which I actually liked.

I was crying so hard that I was streaking my glasses – and I needed to go wash my face.   I went to my vanity and cupped my hands under the running water, refreshing my face a few times with cool water to rinse away the tears and calm the swelling. I reached blindly for the face towel and dried off. Then I started feeling around for my glasses.

They weren't there.

I felt around the vanity top, then got down on the floor, feeling around under the cabinets. My glasses weren't there. I went to check the nightstand next to my bed, in case I had been on auto pilot and placed them there before I washed my face (which made no sense, but it made more sense than glasses evaporating). My glasses were not in my bedroom anywhere.

I went back out to the dining room to see if I had left them there. I cannot see anything without my glasses, so it would have been very strange for me to take them off in the dining room, then blindly make my way to my bedroom to wash my face. In the depths of grief, however, I realized that I could have done just that – removing tear stained lenses to wipe them off, or dry my eyes. It was plausible. Remotely.

My glasses were not in the dining room. They weren't anywhere. I looked for a long time, until I finally gave up and found an old pair in my drawer before I decided to call it a night and try to sleep. Lying in bed, I said out loud in the dark, "Put my glasses back, David."

Silence.

The next morning, I looked again with a fresh effort and fresh eyes. My glasses were nowhere. It was impossible (or at least statistically unlikely) that my glasses had disappeared. I need my glasses to see. I hadn't driven to and from a restaurant, made my way in to my house, found and opened a bottle of wine, and then sat for the next hour, listening to music – never noticing that I couldn't see anything!

There was only one explanation that made any sense to me: David moved them; just like he was moving Mom's glasses. He wanted us to know he was still here.

I wore the old pair of glasses to Cracker Barrel that morning. Quentin and I met Joan for breakfast. After breakfast, I took our iced teas to go, as always, and put them in the console cup holders. I took Quentin to Grandmas, and asked my mother if she would go with me to Costco to look for new glasses (I needed her membership card) and as we rode around in my car, I played David's music.

I shopped around in a few stores for glasses that day, and was not happy about the prospect of coming out-of-pocket two hundred dollars for new ones – when I was sure David had hidden my perfectly good pair. I was getting annoyed. By the time I got home that afternoon, I was fed up with this game.

I looked around the whole house, again – in every room I could have been in the night before. Finally, I'd had enough. This was not amusing. I yelled, "Put my glasses back or I will sage the fuck out of you, David!"

Silence.   Awkward silence.

I suddenly had an urge get something out of my car - and there were my glasses, sitting in the cupholder that had held Cracker Barrel iced teas earlier that morning, in the car I drove around in all day. It was impossible – or statistically unlikely – that they would have been there. It was impossible that I drove around all day with them next to me and no one in my car saw them – and they couldn't have been there because I was able to put drinks in the cupholders.

In my life I have never taken my glasses off in the car, let alone left them there while I wandered blindly in to and around my house all evening.   They hadn't been there until now. This was David – I called his bluff, and he didn't want to get saged.

The next day, we got his personal effects back from the coroner. There on my parent's kitchen table, sat his hat and glasses, a wallet, two shirts and cell phone. The sum total of his belongings.

And then I noticed that his glasses were streaked, as if from tears.

****

Dave's friend has a picture of him, sitting on a beach, frowning.

I asked her if he was being serious in that photo or if he was just making a scowling face to be funny.

She told me, "He was really frowning.
He said he was upset because he knew he should be happy,
but he just couldn't be."

****

Chapter Six
Drink Me

However, she soon made out that she was in a pool of tears
which she had wept when she was nine feet high.
"I wish I hadn't cried so much!" said Alice,
as she swam about, trying to find her way out.

Lewis Carroll, Alice's Adventures In Wonderland – Chapter 2

So here's the thing: I've come to believe that some of us have learned how to raise an antenna so that spirits on the other side can communicate. That's the best way I can put it. I can't necessarily reach out to a certain person, but once the antenna is up, whoever has something to say, generally says it. It used to seem odd to me that I would get messages from people that I hadn't been important to in life – but now I realize that I may be the only one on this side whom they can communicate with from the other side, so they seize the opportunity.

The messages they give are typically pretty clear, usually preceded by something that I could associate them with, in life, to hone me in on who they are – like a smell, or a song… or the sound of a laugh.

The messages are very often for someone, specific. If I do end up sharing a message, it is usually quite meaningful to that person – although it typically means nothing to me.

And… I don't share messages very often.

What bothers most sceptics is the general nature of the messages. After years of receiving and sharing messages from beyond, however, I have come to understand that they do not address earthly concerns, because these concerns don't exist where they now are.

Our secular issues are not relevant on the next plane. It seems to me that they share only enough to spark memories and confirm who they are – to remind us that we once loved, and were loved in return. In the end, that is all that seems to transcend to the next dimension.

I've had the ability to communicate with spirits in other dimensions since I was very young. I have relayed too many accurate messages to grateful loved ones to question my ability, at this point. I have learned how to shut it down - which I usually do. I'm an introvert. It exhausts me just interacting with souls on this plane…

I'm starting to believe, though, that people initially cross over just as they were in life. Some of the confusion and the distortion of perception goes with them, initially, until they can work it out. My brother needed time on the other side, to heal. He needed to learn how to see the light, again.

I don't think my brother crossed over as angry as he was in his final days, however. Newton's law states that energy can never be destroyed, and I know now, at least, that when all of that pain inside somebody is released through suicide, it explodes all over everybody else.

We'll take that hit for you, though, my brother, if it lessens your pain on the other side.

As scientists and practitioners, we can't be so arrogant to believe that we know everything there is to know about the universe, space and time… or that we exist in the only possible dimension. Albert Einstein, who may be the most renowned physicist in history, postulated that time was an illusion – past, present and future are human dimensional constructs. During the Renaissance, Copernicus was radical enough to say that we weren't the center of the universe.

I've had experiences. That's all I can say. I'm limited by language, and words may not accurately express what I have experienced, but there have been visits and messages from the other side. There have been coincidences beyond coincidences of people showing up in my life, right when they need to show up in my life, just to show me I am on the right path. There is something beyond us, and bigger than us, at play out there: I have seen it.

And I'm not the only one who has had these experiences.

We can pass them off as thoughts, as dreams, as illusions - except when they interact with us… When they move things physically.

My Grandmother leaves dimes for us, to let us know she's there. My cousins find them, too, which is why I assume its Gramma Margaret. I find them whenever something major is about to go down, or has just happened. They are not so much of a warning sign, as they are a confirmation that she will be there to support me through it; that I won't stand alone.

David leaves pennies.

Shortly after David died, I had a visit from Grandpa Chet, my dad's father, with whom I hadn't spoken since he passed away in my childhood. He was adamant about wanting my father to know that he was going to be there to greet David when he crossed over. He actually laughed about having to contend with Grandma Margaret for that honor. Apparently, she acquiesced because it was important to him, and he doesn't usually step forward.

Then it struck me: what did he mean, *when* David crossed over? Didn't he already cross over? He had been gone a few days…. The next night, when I heard my brother say, "It's dark here," I was heartbroken for him. I told him he was supposed to go into the light, and that's when he told me there was no light.

I tried to help him, right then. I got into the space where I can most easily access messages from Spirit and the higher power. Often, when I'm in that state, I can see light - not with my eyes but more with my intuition - and the light becomes very bright, very intense. It's not blinding, though, it's comforting.

Usually I see a spot and then focus on it and it's gets bigger - or maybe I just get closer - but this time, when I was trying to access the light, it was like I was seeing a thunderstorm at night, with clouds everywhere, and I could only see flashes of light as behind the clouds.

I could see what looked like a glimmer behind a dark cloud, but as I focused on it, instead of getting stronger, it would just flash a little bit behind the cloud, and then go away. It was almost like I couldn't get to the light, myself, while I was in that space with David.

I even sensed Grandma Margaret on the other side of the light. She was trying to get through to him, but she couldn't reach him. I had a brief moment where I perceived a cloud parting ever-so-slightly and a very, very dark spot going into it.

And then the storm was gone… but I don't know what that dark spot was, and I had no sense of peace that my brother had crossed over successfully. I had a sense that I helped him a little, but I also sensed that he still needed help.

I had a strong feeling that he was caught in a space between the light and the dark, simply because he couldn't see the light – just as he couldn't see it when he was alive. I realized that he may not know how – and that I needed to help him. I didn't know how I was going to do it, but I knew I needed to help him find his light.

A few days later I was at my parents' house when I suddenly smelled smoke.

"What is that smell?" I said.

It was like cigarette smoke – but more caustic. No one in the family smokes, but David did. It was alarming.

I started searching around, looking toward the ceiling. I went outside to see if the roof was on fire – my parents' house had been hit by lightning before – but I saw nothing but blue skies. I came back in, and the smoky smell was so strong that I could barely breathe.

It was burning my throat.

After a moment, I realized that the smoke was emanating from a guitar in the corner - the guitar David had taken with him to the hotel on the beach…the guitar that was with him when he died.

I could almost see smoke billowing around it. I walked closer and the smoky smell got stronger. I said, "Mom! I think David threw a cigarette in the hole of this guitar, and it's been smoldering for days."

I walked over to the guitar, only to discover that the smoke was not coming from inside the guitar. The cloud of smoke was outside the guitar, and I was in the middle of it. I turned around to see David's hat and glasses on the table, directly across from the guitar. The smoke smell was gathering between the three objects.

David.

I moved the hat and glasses to another room. The smoke smell quickly dissipated.

Later that same day, my mom called me and said, "The crematorium just called – David was cremated today,"

"That must have been the smoke we smelled," I said, not sure how my mother would respond.   I knew that I experienced paranormal things, and she knew that I thought I experienced paranormal things, but I didn't think she was ever quite on board with it.

Then she said something that surprised me. "I think that must have been it," she said. And then she added, "I had a similar experience the day Grandma Margaret was cremated."

August 2017

I haven't seen Chris in decades.
We have both moved on to separate lives.
But soul mates come in all packages.

About a week after David died,
Chris called me out of the blue.
"Write your book," he said, "this is your book."

When I called him back,
to tell him that I had decided to write it,
He said, "I just have one question. How can I help?"

I said, "Tell me what you remember about David."

He said, "Well, I remember that I didn't call him David."

"What did you call him?" I asked, confused.

"I called him Little Bob." Chris replied, matter-of-factly.

"Oh Yeah…". I said,
a stirring of a distant memory coming to life…
"Why did you call him that?"

"Because you did!" Chris laughed.

And it all came back to me: I did call him Little Bob.
And my best friend Angie called him Pete. It was a lifetime ago.
Another space and another time.

A memory that had not existed again until just now.

I smiled.

I went back to the posts on the memorial page on Facebook: pictures of my brother in his hat and glasses. They certainly were part of who he was. As I was re-reading all of the memorial posts, it suddenly hit me: my family is posting about David, but everyone else is posting about Dave.

Who the heck was this "Dave" guy?

I called David, 'David'. I scrolled back through messages and posts and text. In every interaction I've had with people since he passed away, I would write about 'David' and his friends would write back about 'Dave'.

Maybe the reason I had not been able to help my brother find the light was because it was not David who needed my help, after all, it was Dave who had succumbed to the darkness– and I didn't know Dave.

****

I drive and listen to the songs he recorded. I relate. I get it.
I never got a chance to hear his music when he was alive.

Tragic.

He was my best friend and I didn't even know him.
Finally, I said, out loud, "I love this song, David."

And I heard him laugh at me.
He said, "Of course you do. That's my worst one."

That seems about right.

****

Chapter Seven
<u>Mad Tea Party</u>

"Do you know,
I always thought unicorns were fabulous monsters, too?
I never saw one alive before!"

"Well, now that we have seen each other," said the unicorn,
"if you'll believe in me, I'll believe in you."

-    *Lewis Carroll, Through the Looking Glass — Chapter 7*

There was light to be found – plenty of it.

On Thursday, June 29, 2017, I posted on Facebook that my brother committed suicide. Within 30 seconds my dad's best friend from Canada called. They haven't seen each other in years. My phone also started ringing. My best friend that I had lost touch with. Friends from Canada that I grew up with.

Chris called - I hadn't spoken to him in years. My ex-husband called too, concerned about our kids and my parents. And he said something very strange: "This wasn't your fault."

So much light in the midst of darkness.

His friend set up a Facebook tribute page for Dave. People were posting and talking and sharing and grieving… and it was the most beautiful human experience I'd ever been part of. I suddenly became a kinder, gentler version of myself.

My darkness was gone.

I read the posts and all I wanted was my brother back, without the darkness - because without the darkness, we could have been best friends. We had so much in common.

The friends who stayed light still saw his authentic self. There were posts with links to his songs, and photos of his painting and drawings that still hang on friends' walls.

Pam posted: Our first roommate bonding we went to bush gardens & rode all the roller coasters. Maybe symbolic of what living with Dave would be like. Our living room was the practice area for his band... He always threw pasta on the wall & declared that's how you know it's cooked.
He was so smart - probably the most intelligent person I've ever met. He had straight As always & made school look effortless. I always thought, he doesn't know his potential.

Mom posted: We've known David for 44 years. He was the sweetest little boy in the world. To us he'll always be our little boy..... the most intelligent, creative, talented, caring, funny, sensitive person in the world. Yes indeed, he did have a unique sense of humor. His greatest passions were his music and his love of animals. We loved him with all our hearts, through all of his ups and downs. I wish I could hold him in my arms right now to tell him everything will be ok. Our family in heaven is waiting with open arms to welcome him home.

Mat posted: I've had this painting of his hanging in every place that I've lived for at least the last 20 years. Currently it's in my den. I remember us finding the frame at a garage sale, with some nature/river landscape print in it. He pulled that out, turned it over, painted this on it and popped it back in the frame. He made a bunch of similar works around that time, though most were smaller. One day, he tossed almost all of them into the dumpster.

> *Ray responded* : That's really amazing!!! He did a whole collection that I got to see that he intended to sell... and the whole entire collection got lost in the mail. That was tragic!!!

I don't think he did anymore after that. We joked that his collection would eventually end up in an art museum and priceless.

Mindy posted: I lived just a couple blocks from him, and soon became a regular at Sunday spaghetti nights. I was always amazed by Dave's creativity and sense of humor. It was never dull with Dave. One Thanksgiving I didn't go home because of the expense. Dave invited me to his parents' house in Altamonte Springs. I declined his invitation, but that evening, he came over with a complete Thanksgiving dinner, all packed away in Tupperware for me. It was one of the nicest things anyone has ever done for me. And that was Dave.

Bill posted: Someone, probably Dave, got a hold of a four-track. After that, everyone began experimenting and recording music.
--We smoked cigarettes and drank beer.
--We listened to music all the time. I was amazed by Dave's depth of knowledge. Thinking about my taste in music – then and now – Dave introduced me to most of my favorite bands. I respected Dave's opinion about music. Although I never let him know this, I held his opinion of music (and most things) above that of anyone else.
--I also remember how Dave encouraged everyone to play music. No matter how poorly I played, I never felt him judge or ridicule me. Regretfully, I lost touch with Dave after college. I moved away and it was just hard enough to stay in contact that I didn't. I never had the experience of Dave pushing me away. I didn't see much of the depression. I'm lucky.

Cindy posted: Rip cousin David! My memories of you are mostly of a young boy. I hadn't seen much if you through the later years!! The memories are of a very cool comical kid!! I was much older then you. I just wish we could have gotten a chance to talk again in our later years....You will be sadly missed by many people. Give Grandma Margaret and my Dad and everybody all our our Love.. Now you and Uncle George can do some guitar jammin'!! Until we meet again. Love your Cousin Cindy.

Carol posted: RIP David. Though distance prevented me from knowing you, I thought of you often. I will meet you in another place and time.

Lori posted: Good bye , cousin... I'm struggling with what to say at this moment, but all I can say is I'm sad...Though it had been quite a long time since I'd seen you just know that I will miss you...My wonderful memories of you have never faded, I have thought of them, often...I will cherish them and like the rest of us wished there were more. Give my dad and grandma Margaret a big hug from me ...Until all of us are reunited... play with my dog, Verdel, too (he's the white and tan shiatzu) ...

Jodee posted: Yesterday Lincoln Square Presbyterian had our service to honor Dave's life and to pray for him and his family. It was moving to hear so many people stand up and tell stories about Dave and how much they miss seeing him each Sunday and how generous and kind he was to everyone. Dave made everyone sound good. He showed up early every Sunday and was the best engineer we ever had. We miss him so much.

Armando posted his performance of a re-worded Travis cover: The Cage - For Dave Rest in peace brother. I am better for knowing you! And thank you all for your gift of David to us.

> You broke the bread
> We drank the wine
> Your lip was bleedin' but it was fine
> Come on inside, babe, across the line
> I love you more than I
>
> But then this bird just flew away
> He was never meant to stay
> Oh to keep him caged would just delay the spring

You broke your word
Now that's a lie
We had a deal that you would try
Come on inside, now, I think it's time
High time we drew the line

But then this bird just flew away
While I looked the other way
Oh to keep him caged would just delay the spring₃

Andy posted: One of my favorite things about (our band) was the banter between Dave and Brian, and the looney show biz antics…

I saw glimmers of light in people's accounts of his interactions with them over the years. David still existed, all this time.

I was confused.

After years of dismissing him as succumbing to the dark side, I discovered that Anakin was still in there! I had not been able to see his light for so many years. I gave up trying, and he wouldn't have shown it to me, anyhow.

I poured through the Facebook posts: wonderful things written about a cherished friend. Artists, expressing themselves beautifully and meaningfully.

This was light.

****

July 17, 2017

Dave: Well how about you forgive yourself and I'll forgive myself?

Me: Okay.

*Me: You know, I'm sensing that it's getting a little brighter
where you are.*

Dave: Yeah, it is. I can see where I'm flicking my cigarettes, now.

****

Chapter Eight
<u>Painting the Roses Red</u>

"It's a poor sort of memory that only works backwards,"
says the White Queen to Alice."

— *Lewis Carroll, Through the Looking Glass – Chapter 5*

Sometime during his last few days on Earth, Dave took his paintings off of my parents' walls. He had always hated that they had his art up everywhere. Borderline self-loathing. In his rage over the argument with my father, Dave took all of his artwork down. After he died, my mother went to put the paintings back on the wall, and discovered that he had scribbled all over them, with a black sharpie.

When his friend came to the house after the funeral, she noticed that on one of them, it wasn't just scribbles: it was the word, "MINE."

After my parents realized that the paintings were defaced, my dad went to get David's painting portfolio out of the back room to replace them – and that's when they realized that David had taken the portfolio with him.

Borderline retaliation: you withheld something from me, now I'll withhold everything of me from you.
The portfolio wasn't among his belongings sent back from the coroner, however. Sadly, as his friend told them later, she and Dave had stopped at Starbucks on their way to the beach, and she had seen him throw something away in the dumpster out back. She said it was flat, the size of a portfolio – but she did not realize at the time that it was all of his paintings.

When she realized what had transpired, his friend rushed back to the Starbucks to check the dumpster, but it had been days... Dave's paintings were gone. Forever. Just like his collection of paintings that had been lost in the mail.

Ray told me recently that he doesn't think Dave would have been Dave without being a borderline. That surprised me a bit. Ray is a mental health professional – and it was not an uninformed opinion. Ray said he believes that the experience of the disorder was paramount to his artistic gifts - and if he hadn't had that experience, he wouldn't be as talented.

I rejected that theory, for a moment. Here I had believed that the disorder kept him from his potential. After talking to Ray, I realized that the heightened sensitivity to interpersonal angst, and the experience of suffering, *would have been* what made Dave the musician and artist he was. It honed his talent. I began to think about all of the artists and musicians who were also likely borderlines, in regard to all of the recently publicized suicides.

It seems that borderlines can take their intense sensitivities and feelings of emptiness and either shut down and wallow in self-pity, or they can transfer it into art. The high number of suicides among artists and musicians may be correlated to borderline pathology. Of course, the likelihood of being able to funnel that energy in to a creative outlet depends on higher level of intelligence or ability. Not all borderlines will be gifted artists, but borderlines who are gifted artists certainly have an outlet for their extreme pain and sensitivity.

Heightened sensitivity often links us to a higher power. Altered states of consciousness can connect us with source, which, in turn, heightens creativity. But what if the heightened sensitivity connects someone to a dark source, instead of a light source - so they experience a higher consciousness, but in a Twisted, dark way.

After my brother's cremation, my father threw himself into my master suite remodel project. I was purchasing bead board and a vanity and crown molding and decorative ceiling tiles - and the pressure was on with all of the construction materials piling up in my garage. I throw myself into creative projects when I'm in pain, as well.

Aidan and my father spent about two weeks on the remodel project. It was a necessary distraction for everyone. We had started painting my room before David died… which is what kept my mother from rushing home that fateful day.

My Dad's original plan was for David to help with the remodel, and that he and David and Aidan could have some bonding time.

But things went south… and that was never to be.

Turning my bedroom into a construction zone meant no one could find anything when they needed it. Pencils went missing, nails went missing. On the first day of the project, I found a penny on the floor. I picked it up and put it on top of the dresser. The next day I heard my Dad sputter because he couldn't find his pencil. I went in to help – and there was the penny on the step stool. I asked Aidan why they had put the penny on the step stool.

He looked at me like I had two heads, and said "Why would we put a penny on the step stool?"

I moved it to my dresser, again.

Throughout the remodeling project, the only thing that did not get lost was that penny. They had to go back to Home Depot to replace missing nails and screws, but that penny just hung around. Finally, after all of the molding was up, and fixtures were set, and the project was done, I set the Roomba robot vacuum loose on my bedroom floor, to get rid of the remaining signs of construction dust. After it was done with the room and turned itself off, I went to go put the vacuum on the charger – and there, in the middle of the floor, sat the penny.

It was statistically unlikely that it had not been sucked up by the robot vacuum – or that it was still there at all.

I put the penny on my vanity and took a picture of it with my phone.

The next time I looked, the penny was gone.

****

Frantic Message to Ray, 7/5/17

Me: Hi Ray! My dad accidentally cancelled David's SoundCloud account because he didn't know what it was, and it was a recurring charge. Did you, by any chance, get everything downloaded off of SoundCloud? My dad is really upset because he didn't realize what he was doing.

Ray: It's still there!!! I'll download what I can now.

Ray: Ok, so they started disappearing, but I got all the good stuff... I think I got 90% of everything. 88 tracks.

Me: Thank you!!

Ray: Get me your address and I'll send 'em over. I still have to pick up a usb, but the songs are safe.

****

In listening to David's music, and to his songs with Ray and Mondo's band, *Claudio*, I have really become a fan. My favorite of Dave's originals is *Everybody's Such an Asshole*. It's actually a nice little song – catchy tune, with a sentiment we can all relate to, at some time or another.

What's poignant is that my brother didn't just relate to the song, he lived it. To me it is the perfect little snapshot inside a borderline head.

Dave played every instrument himself, as he did on all of his tracks, and sang the lyrics. It's a good song.

He also recorded an album of 80s covers. The first thing I noticed when I looked at the titles was that the play list read like a suicide note: Always Something There to Remind Me, Don't You Forget About Me, If You Were Here, Don't Dream It's Over. He laid down the tracks with happy little tunes and a very dark haunting vocal - almost like he was mocking the casual listener, knowing they have no idea of the darkness they are tapping their foot to.

"Sardonic", as my friend Cathi called it.

My favorite Dave 80s cover was of "If You Were Here," by the Thomson Twins. I knew it as the song from the final scene in Sixteen Candles. Dave always changed the lyrics of his covers to reflect his own experience. These, in particular, break my heart:

> *The rainwater drips through the cracks in my ceiling.*
> *And I'll need to take some time to repair.*
> *But just like the rain, I will always be falling...*
> *Just as I rise, and fall, again.*

Ray said that Dave played each instrument and layered the recordings, but not in a straightforward way. He said it was like

Dave was playing different songs and merging them together, sometimes playing melodies backward. He layered his own voice tracks– and the effect was, at times, "creepy".

Sardonic.

Art.

Dave's friends were artists – and they appreciated Dave's gifts in a way that many of the rest of us couldn't. Dan said that in their youth, Dave exposed him to things he had never been exposed to before. Dave was an artistic genius, and he was brilliant.

Dave's functional skills were never what they needed to be, however. Borderlines often cannot hold down jobs, and in retrospect, Dave never could. Dan said he got Dave a job as a bar back when he first moved to Chicago, but Dave was off the schedule within a month. When I was in college, my friend, Angie, got him a summer job at the local triple-A ball field, where he worked with her and Chris. I never knew this, but Dan said he had to pick Dave up at the ball field a few times, because he couldn't make it through a shift.

I also remember he worked at SeaWorld for one day when he was in high school - and walked out after a few hours because the supervisor asked him to push garbage down with his hand.

No, he was never on the path to be a working adult. The question remains, though, did drugs make it worse?

According to Dan, Dave was still Dave when they were all just smoking pot. Progressive use of heavier drugs appeared to exacerbate Dave's descent into Madness. I now know that Dave was routinely using some pretty hard-core drugs after high school, and by the time he finally joined Dan in Chicago, things went south fairly quickly.

The other catalyst into full-blown borderline personality disorder was the alliance with his new girlfriend - who moved to Chicago

94

with him and later become his wife. It was after he met her that the allegations of family abuse started to flourish.

From my perspective, they were out of nowhere. All I know is that he had an enabling partner who reinforced his complaints of being mistreated throughout his life – and having audience reinforced the stories until the memories of abuse became real to him. According to Dan, she was enamored with Dave the artist, and was more than happy to enable and sympathize with the victim.

Dan told me that he also believed Dave's allegations of a history of neglect and maltreatment, because that's what friends do – until he met my family and spent time with us, and realized that we were also just victims of the borderline darkness.

****

My great aunt passed away shortly after David died. My mom's family loved pie – and on the day of our aunt's passing, relatives were posting on Facebook that they hoped there would be pie in heaven for Aunt Theresa. That afternoon I wrote lyrics to a song: "Pie in Heaven". My dad wrote the music and by that evening, my parents, sons, Joan and I were all singing it around the table – while Aidan's girlfriend video recorded it for Facebook. Our friends and relatives loved it.

Several weeks later, my cousins Cindy, Carol and Lori came down from New York for a special memorial service at our aunt's church. I didn't find this out until we arrived at the church, but my mother had volunteered us to sing *Pie in Heaven* for the congregation. I couldn't believe it: What on earth was she thinking??? And there was no getting out of it when the minister introduced us to come on stage.

I took the lead because I had to. I started singing, eyes focused nervously on one spot in the back of the room, not knowing how the church members were going to respond to our irreverent song about pie in heaven. Then, I looked over at my family. They were all singing and smiling at me. I realized that we weren't singing for the church, we were singing for each other, and for Great Aunt Theresa, and for all of our pie-loving family on the other side - and I felt their presence there. I felt love. This was light.

When we got home I knocked over my purse. Out fell a bunch of dimes...

They liked the song.

One afternoon, while my cousins were still visiting, Cindy told Carol and I that she had a dream shortly after David died, in which she was walking toward the ocean on an empty beach.

She said she had never been to that beach in her dream before, but that she wanted to go see the ocean sometime during this trip to Florida. She said that, in her dream, she felt an overwhelming feeling of, "I finally made it!" She said that phrase kept running through her mind, over and over in the dream: "I finally made it."

I finally made it

I asked her what the beach looked like. She pulled out her phone and showed me a picture she found that resembled the beach in her dream. I looked at the sand and the dunes with the billowy beach grasses.

It looked like Ormond Beach, where David died.

Cindy hadn't seen David for years. She was older than him by several years – and, while she and I were close, she had only really known my brother as a child.

She did not know that David had passed away at a beach.

I pulled up the website gallery pictures from his hotel, featuring the beach. "That's the place in my dream." she said.

I finally made it.

Cindy had a dream about the beach where her cousin passed away, without even knowing it. As we three cousins let that sink in, we started to believe that she had picked up on what David had been feeling in that moment - when he realized he did not have to wake up, this time.
Cindy said she had felt the need to go to the beach ever since she had the dream. We took a road trip to the coast, and had drinks and lunch at a beach bar overlooking the dunes and the ocean – and Carol went with Cindy to walk on the sand.

And they felt very happy about that.

We're getting there, David... there is so much light.

How can I help you see it?

****

Stray Dog Recording Studio post, 2016

Here's some 'wisdom' I've gained about engineering/ recording, for anyone starting out, or thinking about it:

Over these many years of doing this shit, I've developed certain etiquette/ social/ communication-skills/ tricks/ methods for dealing with musicians who come over to work with me.

I'm usually able to establish a good rapport fairly quickly to make folks feel 'at home'/ comfortable.

I've been lucky to have worked with all kinds of folks, and I've found that I'm able to get along with everybody.

...I always like to say: "Somehow, I have a knack for making people feel comfortable when they come over to work with me, whereas everywhere else I go, I tend to make people uncomfortable"...

-Dave

****

One of the friends who had been blown off the path was Brian, his former band mate from high school and college. A former band member posted that one his favorite memories of the band had been the banter between Dave and Brian. Whatever happened to that friendship? I did know that Brian was one of the people who went dark to Dave, and I had heard about Dave lashing out at him in very strange ways. I assumed I would not hear from Brian, and that piece of this puzzle would remain unknown.

To my surprise, Brian did reach out to me, after I posted that I wanted to write a book. He sent an email that was so raw and full of truth – a brilliant account of the last days of Dave. He needed his own story told, and seemed to really want me to understand Dave's descent into Madness, from an insider's perspective. Brian said to contact him if I ever wanted to talk.

According to Brian, Dave started taking copious amounts of drugs around the same time as his initial suicide attempt. His email was too raw to paraphrase. With permission, I have decided to cite excerpts.

> *...Andy and I talked about it and our takeaway with that drug was that it turned the nicest person into the surliest shittiest angriest drunk person you can imagine.*

> *All of us wanted to do something, didn't know what to do, weren't equipped/too young to say whatever the right things might have been. Finally, Matt said, "You're really starting to scare me, Dave." We all nodded and voiced agreements.*

> *I'll never forget this. Dave just said, "No offense, but I don't give a fuck."*

> *Dave drunk and on roofies was like an entirely different person, but a person it seems we would all get to know better, sadly. (That was probably the person you had dinner with on his birthday.)*

> *...I think I saw Dave maybe five times in the past seventeen years. There was a point I stopped hating him, but the effort*

to try and patch things up seemed so exhausting and it also felt like that ship had sailed long ago. I had my own life in Chicago and he had his. It was horrible watching from afar that descent get worse and worse as the years passed. The end of their marriage. His posts on social media.

...About a year and a half ago I ran into him at a show. He wasn't drinking, seemed ok, almost his old self, was there to "try and meet chicks." I offered to buy him a beer, he told me he wasn't drinking then offered to buy me one, a small example of the innate generosity he had towards all his friends. He was lucid. He talked politics, still had that active and unique mind, that barbed humor. But it wasn't all there. He wanted to re-record all the old band songs with me, songs we hadn't played in twenty years. It was his attempt to reach out, but it felt sad and exactly what it would have been-- middle-aged men trying to relive their youth.

And what felt the most sad to me, and I think you made a reference to this when you last saw him, was that he seemed the same in a way you don't want an old friend to be the same. Like he was still that 18 year old, only now in a 43 year old body. Calling women "chicks," for instance. A time maybe a year after that when I ran into him and he had been drinking, he tried to make some snide comment at my expense like he might have done when we were much younger. It was too sad to have any real reaction.

It took a long time for me to grasp the mental health side of what Dave suffered. There was so much drug use going on with him that I now would understand was self-medication, but I also was much more inclined to ascribe the drug and alcohol abuse to what I perceived to be his lack of coping skills or jekyll/hyde behaviors. I know it didn't help, obviously, but understand just how deep all of this was.

I'm glad he had friends who stuck by him like we had before we could no longer deal with it for these last few years. I was shocked yet pleasantly surprised to discover that he had developed a relationship with a church in his neighborhood--never would have seen that coming.

I shared a lot of the great memories on the fb page. I certainly didn't intend for this to become a fucking Russian novel, and furthermore, if it comes off as an airing of grievances, that really was not my intention...

I also remember how cool it was when Dave had an apartment with you when we were just starting out at UCF. There was so much I learned from Dave, about myself, about the world, good and bad lessons.

As I said in the fb page, there's always some joke from that time that maybe only me and him, or me, Dave, and Dan found to be hilarious that passes through my mind on any given day.

We can talk about anything else when you're ready to do so. I really didn't mean to go on for this long. Christ. Sorry.

Give my best to your parents and your family, --Brian

When his friends tried to confront him about drug use, he would have taken that as an attack, as a borderline – and he countered defensively: "No offense, but I don't give a fuck." What they would not have realized at the time, was that it was probably a turning point for him – the moment they went dark. It was the beginning of the end for them – he would never let them know him, again.

According to Brian, Dave never forgave the friends who signed the Baker Act to have him committed after his first suicide attempt. After I got him out of the facility, Brian apparently tried to convince my parents not to drop him back off at the apartment. The problem is, my parents wouldn't have known a different option. They didn't have all the facts, or a roadmap. Even knowing what we know now, there was little they could have done differently. David was completely denying the event as a suicide attempt and was insistent that he was a victim of a misguided 911 call.

Also, David was not just a depressed drug user who would stop when he felt better. He was a borderline, self-medicating, although none of us comprehended that at the time. As such, David was not someone who tolerated withholding: he was an adult, and if he wanted to go back to his apartment, he would get there come hell or high water, with no regard for personal safety.
My parents really had no choice but to take him back to his apartment.

Shortly before Dave left Chicago to move back to Florida, he showed up at a venue where Brian was performing and made a scene. Dave ruined the show and had to be removed. That was when Brian called Dan and asked him to contact Dave's parents. Seems to me that Brian may have been an unsung hero in this drama. My guess is that the reason he went so dark to Dave is because he actually did try to help over the years. He did try to confront Dave about his behavior at various points... and, as I've said before, confronting a borderline with reality is like throwing holy water on a vampire.

****

Kelly and I sat at my dining room table and drank wine and poured through Brian's email. She honed-in on the same line that had resonated with me: "he seemed the same… in a way you don't want an old friend to be the same."

We read that again together. Kelly sipped some more wine. She mused over it. Finally, she said "Let me see the video, again." We watched a video of Dave that Ray posted. Dave was sputtering and complaining through a song that Armando was singing, because he didn't like it. Kelly observed: "He made the experience about himself. He's just as you described him, and he appears very eccentric."

That's when it really made sense: he was not a different person around Ray, it's just that Ray and his brother got the best of him, and appreciated it. Even when he was helping someone else, though, his orientation was on himself.
It doesn't mean he's wasn't a generous and loving friend, but his focus would have been limited to his own experience. His disorder didn't prevent him from being kind and excessively giving to those he valued and trusted. Ray and Armando were allowed access: They saw the real Dave.

And they loved him, anyhow.

Dave was apparently still fun to be around. Funny. Entertaining. Crude, but guys in bands are used to that. And he was relevant enough that even the people who were blown away reached out to me to tell his story.

In recent photos, Dave looked like he felt lonely, even in a crowd. There are times when most of us can relate to that feeling.... but my brother was lonely even when he was in a crowd of people who loved him unconditionally... who shared common interests...

It's never enough for a borderline... the feeling of being loved doesn't last because of that dreadful hole in them... you can pour it in, but it just flows back out. Down the drain it goes.

A vessel continuously filled, but always empty...

It seems that even God's love flows out of that hole. How desperately painful that must be – to be so profoundly and continuously separated from Source.

I have been heartbroken; we all have. Gramma Margaret said to me once, "Heartbreak is the worst kind of hurt." She knew heartbreak all too well. Gramma had a real soft spot for David – she must have sensed his emptiness.

When I've been heartbroken, it didn't matter who else loved me - it didn't take the pain away. No matter who spent time with me, the heartache was ever present, maybe suppressed, but always coiled and ready to spring back to the forefront. Dave was heartbroken from his divorce and the loss of his dogs... but there was a hurt that existed independent of that.... one caused by his distorted perceptions that *everyone* had hurt him... with the exception of a few people who remained light, for whatever reason.

The hardest thing for me when I was reading the Facebook posts was being confronted with the idea that there was a Dave that existed, who I didn't know. A best friend who I had never met. I had believed, in those final years, that he was just darkness, and that belief was what justified and perpetuated our lack of relationship. The posts made me wonder if I was just wrong: that he was only crazy around me. If I actually brought it out in him.

After sorting through everything thus far, I realized that he was a borderline, and that was true in every situation of his life, manifesting itself in different ways, but still present. He was disordered. He was the tragic character in his own book.

Dave was fundamentally and inescapably Dave, and there were plenty of people who loved him, anyway.

Now the realization: it wasn't *his* light I needed to find – it was the light he was surrounded with in life; the light he couldn't see in the people around him, just as he couldn't see the light when he crossed over.

He was surrounded by people who loved him - but he didn't see that. He never could. The light of love couldn't penetrate the darkness when he was alive, and it couldn't now.

But love is light...
I realized, all of a sudden, that if I could help him to see that love, he would see that light, and he could finally be at peace.

I realized, I actually could help him.

I needed to meet these people - these friends of my brothers, who I had never met. The friends of a man I didn't know.

I needed to seek them out – those people who saw Dave's human frailty and loved him, anyhow. I needed to help him see the light that had always been surrounding him.

And I needed to finally meet Dave.

****

Facebook post, July 26, 2017

Me:

I am on a journey to meet "Dave".
I only knew "David"...
and he was gone years ago.
I booked a flight to Chicago August 11th through 14th.
If you knew Dave and have stories or insights
that you are willing to share, please private message me.
I believe his is a story that needs to be heard and it needs to be told.

****

Chapter Nine
Down the Rabbit Hole

"Would you tell me, please, which way I ought to go from here?"
(Alice speaks to Cheshire Cat)
"I don't much care where-" said Alice.

"Then it doesn't matter which way you go," said the Cat.
"--so long as I get somewhere," Alice added as an explanation.

"Oh, you're sure to do that," said the Cat,
"if you only walk long enough."

Alice felt that this could not be denied, so she tried another question.
"What sort of people live about here?"

"In that direction," the Cat said, waving its right paw round, "lives a Hatter: and in that direction," waving the other paw, "lives a March Hare. Visit either you like: they're both mad."

"But I don't want to go among mad people," Alice remarked.

"Oh, you can't help that," said the Cat: "we're all mad here. I'm mad. You're mad."

"How do you know I'm mad?" said Alice.

"You must be," said the Cat, "or you wouldn't have come here."

— *Lewis Carroll, Alice's Adventures in Wonderland, Chapter 6*

I leave for Chicago in a couple days. My sons are proud of me. Everyone at work is so supportive. My friends have expressed awe. My parents haven't said anything.

I can't read how they feel about it. My parents and I are having different experiences with this. They lost a child, and there is no emotion I could have that would compare to that.

The day before I left, my co-worker, Khakie, came into my office. She stood there hesitating for a moment, and then said, "Please be careful in Chicago."

I smiled at her. "Are you worried?" I asked.

She said, "Yes. Because you're going alone, and you don't know these people you're going to see."

I laughed. "I know," I said, "I'm going to see people who were friends with a crazy person..."

I wasn't afraid, though. I never do anything by myself – putting myself alone in unchartered waters is something I simply won't do. I don't even like meeting someone in an unfamiliar restaurant.

There was something very comforting about the messages from his Chicago friends, however. Every Sunday for the past few years, Dave had provided the sound engineering for a church. He had met the pastor's wife in the courtyard of his studio-slash-apartment, that was shared with the church's business office.

My parents received cards and letters from members of the congregation, and I was sent private messages. They posted pictures on his memorial page of the private service they held for him in someone's back yard – a guitar propped by a tree. And they posted that it was so nice to finally meet Armando, who had apparently gone by himself to honor Dave. Dave had said there was nothing 'Mondo wouldn't do for him.

Maybe he was right.

Even that video of one of his final recording sessions that Kelly and I watched made me want to meet the people in his life. The way friends treated him in the video was heartwarming. In the video, when Dave was going off about not liking the song, Armando looked at him with such kindness… and he laughed, the way Quentin did when David went off on him. I recognized that laugh. It was a laugh of connectedness – of appreciation. And when Armando laughed, Dave wasn't offended.

I am so happy that he had these people in his life. I couldn't wait to meet as many of them as I could.

But who the heck was Chuck?

****

Stray Dog Recording Studio post, continued

--- Another "trick" ...Just outta self preservation, cuz I got (really-fucking) sick of crash-cymbals getting smashed right by my head while I was mic'ing up snare drums:

An early 'strategy' I came up with for dealing with this 'problem' was to say to the drummer (once his kit was set-up, but he wouldn't step away from his 'throne'- like all drummers):

"Can I see your drum sticks really quick?" -- And as soon as they handed em over, I'd say "Thanks.", and put em straight into my back pocket ... It got the point across, but it also made me come across as pretty dick-y.

Now, what I do is: After load in, after we figure out how to arrange everyone in the room, I say:

"OK, so what I usually do is get out of your guys' way while you set up your instruments, and get comfortable in your space. Once you're ready, let me know. I'll ask you to "take-five", and go chill in the control room while I move in and set up the mic's and stuff. Otherwise, it's a bit of a cluster-fuck."

-Works like a charm. Problem solved. Everyone 'gets it' and appreciates the idea. And I don't come across like a prick.

****

When I was about 10 years old, my brother gave me a giant stuffed bear that he won the carnival because I was sad that I couldn't win one... but he was never able to win one again for himself.

Not ever.

And that *was* the metaphor...

He was generous to a fault, but he could never win for himself.

Maybe I just wanted to go win him a giant bear.

So, I found myself on a flight to Chicago. By myself. I posted about it on Facebook the night before, and was touched by the outpouring of support and love from friends, and family, and strangers alike.

That morning, I waited until my boys left for high school at 6:15 am to finalize packing and get on the road to the airport. They had just started back to school after the summer - it was the second day of classes for them. I made them coffees to go and hugged them goodbye as they walked out the door.

My friend, Allie, picks them up and takes them to school every morning, along with her son, Alec. I actually could take them to school with my new work schedule, but it's tradition for Miss Allie to take them. Our sons met in kindergarten, became Eagle Scouts together, play guitar together, and suddenly, they are high school seniors together.

Quentin said that on the first day of classes, one of his teachers asked him if he was Aidan and Alec's little brother... Quentin just said, "yes". Family is not always biological.

People often ask Allie and I if we are sisters. I had assumed that people thought we were related because our sons spent so much time together, acted like brothers and looked like they could be fraternal twins. One day, however, we ran into each other at the vet's office, with no kids, and the woman behind the counter asked if we were sisters. It threw me off guard. Why would saying hello to someone suggest that we were sisters?

Clearly it is the way we interact that makes us family. I feel like Dave had that with Ray, in the end. There are some bonds of friendship that forever change us... Some connections that are transcendent... Some people who love who we are on the inside, regardless of how we act on the outside.

There is something afoot here in this Dave community I have become a part of... an instant, unshakable bond... There is light here, Dave. I can see it.

****

I hate to fly. I never was afraid to fly until I became a mother. At that instant, I had everything to lose. The night before my flight, I put my life insurance policy information on my dresser. I felt like I was going on a journey through the looking glass... and for the first time I was aware of the possibility that I may not return – at least not the way I left.

On the flight up, there were no tv screens at the seats... we had to use our phones connected to wi-fi to watch movies and tv. Flying used to be an elite mode of travel – now it's just a bus in the sky.

I asked the flight attendant for earbuds and he wasn't sure he had any, and said he was going to check. After a few minutes went by, and the flight attendant didn't return, the man next to me offered me an unused free pair he had from a prior flight.... it was an unsolicited act of human kindness. Not a major act, just a flicker of light.

On the flight home, a man in line said to me, "Looks like you picked a good flight." I looked up and saw that it was the same guy. A different book would have been a love story. That would have been a really good book. And the second meeting would have been saved for the end… but, instead, it's here in the middle. A flash of human light – but not a main character.

In this book, he got on the plane to Orlando and I got on the plane to Orlando, we didn't sit together, and as far as I know, I've never seen him again. I have no memory of what he looks like.

And it is statistically unlikely that he will ever read this book.

****

I stayed at a hotel overlooking Lincoln Park. I chose that hotel because it had a rooftop bar. I figured it would be a nice place to meet up and talk – and if I get to Chicago and no one wants to meet me after all, at least I will have somewhere nice to sit, by myself.

On the first morning, I got up very early. I went to the lobby to get some tea, but the café wasn't open yet. I walked out into the cool morning (it's cool in Chicago when you're from Florida – even in the summer) and crossed over to the park where an incredible farmers market was setting up.

They weren't quite ready yet, so I walked into the park. I took some gorgeous pictures of the flowers and the scenery. I was amazed by the beautiful gardens. Even coming from Florida, which is blooming all year, I was still in awe of the colors.

And then, all of a sudden, quite unexpectedly, I came across a kangaroo.

And then a lion...

"Well," I thought, "that's a curious thing to find in a park at 6am!"

"Hello, Lion." I said. The lion sat regally on his rock, alone, unphased by my presence. It was just he and I. I realized that this must be the famous Lincoln Park Zoo... although how it was possible to wander in to such a place before hours, with no gate or fanfare, I had no idea. The zoo was apparently closed, but the animals were all out. I had never been to a zoo before where all of the animals were out and present and perched so perfectly in their habitats.

It was just me in the zoo, with the exception of some early morning walkers, who would emerge quickly, one at a time - specifically dressed in what were clearly walk-enhancing clothes - and then disappear. As I walked around, taking pictures of animals and flowers, one of the early morning walkers came by, all decked out in her white walking garb, and said, "Would you like to see some polar bears?"

I said, "Who wouldn't?"

She laughed and said, "They're right next to the plexiglass this morning – just around the corner," and away she walked. Here one minute, gone the next – like she was late for something...

I walked around the bend, and there they were: polar bears, a mere six inches away from me – and there was no one else around to bother them away. It was just me and them, and we were all fine with that. It was like I had a whole park and the zoo to myself. I was certainly through the looking glass, here.

After a while, I made my way back to the hotel through the farmers market - which was so wonderful that I had to take pictures for my little chef, Quentin. Also at the park that weekend was the Chicago hot dog festival, hosted by the Historical Society, and I found myself talking to all sorts of characters as I walked around.

Joan loves Chicago hot dogs. Aidan loves history. Mom and Dad love David. I found myself wishing I was not so alone, there, in Wonderland.

****

In too deep,
Your spirit's flyin'
You've been down into that Rabbit Hole
You sneak deep inside my eyes.

-Heavyset,
original song by "Claudio"
Recorded at Stray Dog Studios

****

Armando

Armando took the last known picture of Dave. It was taken just before he left Chicago. He took Dave to a Mexican restaurant in Lincoln Square and they sat outside on the patio. Armando said that the whole time they were out there, people were walking by saying hello to Dave. He was apparently well-known in that area. Armando said that they seemed to be mostly people from the church. The way Armando described it, it seemed like a pleasant afternoon. In the photo, Dave sat with his arms folded looking off into the distance.

That photo is now displayed on the front of the box that holds Dave's ashes.

Armando met me at the rooftop bar, after work on Friday. It took him two hours to drive through traffic. Ray had said: "Armando's easy to find: look for the world's tallest Mexican." Armando came in wearing a newsboy cap. We sat and talked for hours, drinking the bar's signature drink: Mexican spritzers. At check-in, I was given coupons for two free Mexican spritzers – so it became our drink of the evening.

We got into a conversation about perceptions, and how borderlines tend not to do well in therapy because they would have to accept that much of their reality was actually a misperception. Like the Matrix. Suddenly I said, "What if it was me the whole time? What if it were my perceptions that were distorted?"

Armando said, "What if you're not here at all. What if you're home talking to yourself in the mirror?" and validated my Through the Looking-Glass metaphor without even knowing of it.

I said, "Actually, that would be more likely than me having flown to Chicago by myself sitting here with you right now," as I found myself no longer in the Orlando, but instead sitting with a very good-looking young man in a cap, drinking Mexican spritzers at a rooftop bar in Lincoln Park.

Here I was in topsy-turvy world – talking to my new friend about my late brother. I wondered if Dave was there, with us. He never would have participated in this event in life, but having gone through the looking glass, were we all here, together?

It was a nice evening. Armando truly is a good guy. Dave once said that he thought that Mondo would do anything for him, and he was right. He sat with Dave's middle-aged sister in a rooftop bar, listening and talking - and he even picked up the tab. He just didn't want Ray to find out he was drinking "Mexican spritzers."

The next day he came by and drove me up to Lincoln Square to see Dave's apartment and Studio. We pulled up in front of some old storefronts with For Lease signs on them. Next to one of them was a small alley with an iron gate. He turned the car off and said, "We're here!"

I was confused. "Where are we?" I said.

"Stray Dog," Armando replied.

I didn't see anything that looked like a studio or even a business, not to mention an apartment. He said, "It's down there," and pointed to the gate in front of the alley.

He asked me if I had called Jodee from the church before we came. I looked up and noticed a sign that said, "Church Office", under the For Lease sign in the window. I had not called Jodee. I forgot that he had asked me if I was in touch with her, and suggested at the rooftop bar that I call her to see if she could have the landlord let us in to Dave's old place. Too many Mexican spritzers. I also thought it would have been an imposition. I thought I was imposing on everyone too much, already. I thought I could just look at Dave's studio from the outside, and that would be enough.

I walked up the step and tried the church office door. It was locked. The blinds were drawn, but Armando cupped his eyes close to the glass and realized there was someone in there. He knocked on the door, and to my surprise, she opened it. Armando introduced me as Dave's sister. She greeted me and said she was sorry for my loss. She knew exactly who I was because Jodee had said that I was coming to the Sunday service the next day.

Armando asked if there was any way she could contact the landlord or Jodee, to see if we could get in the gate. I was so glad he took control of the situation because I suddenly fell quiet. I felt like a subdued version of myself, suddenly overcome with reverence for the situation. It had been a magical trip so far, my journey to Wonderland, but the surreal became palpable as I found myself near where my brother had lived, with people who had known him there.

I walked outside and looked at the gate, and that's when I saw the Stray Dog Recording Studio sticker on the gate - and a handwritten note that my brother had taped below it, providing directions to the postman for package delivery. For the first time during this trip I felt very, very sad. The reality of why I was there was sinking in all of a sudden: my brother had committed suicide.

Everything had been so exciting, up to this point. This moment was somber.

The woman came out and said she couldn't reach Jodee, but said that she thought we could go through the back door of the church office and get to his apartment. She graciously led us through the church office and out the back. I found myself in a small courtyard where Armando said they had many, many good times - sitting around smoking and drinking in between recording sessions.

We walked up to his door and looked in. We were able to see into the studio, where Dave lived and recorded music. It seemed so isolated. I could see it being lonely. I felt lonely there. Armando

120

suggested that because it had to be soundproofed, with the windows covered, it would have been even more isolating. The sunlight couldn't come in. Maybe that explains why I perceived so much darkness around him.

Now that the studio was empty, the landlord had removed the soundproofing from the windows and I was able to get a full view of the space: two rooms and a hallway ... and the kitchen/bathroom that I couldn't see. I did feel like he had good times there, but I also felt an overwhelming sense of sadness emanating from some of the spaces. I felt like I knew exactly where the suicide attempts occurred, but I got the distinct impression that his last moments there were happy ones.

Armando said that Dave had been very hopeful about moving to Florida and starting a new future. He said that on the day he was helping him move out, Dave found a penny face-up on the ground, and thought it was a good sign.

A penny. Like the penny that had been showing up at my house.

Now existing on another plane, it seems that Dave would have known that I would be having this conversation with Armando – or had already had it, somewhere in the time-space continuum – and knew that I would connect the penny to him. The penny was him letting me know he was there. He was on the journey, too.

I asked Armando to take a picture of me in front of the door with the Stray Dog sticker on it, and I started to smile - but then stopped myself before he took the picture. Armando asked, "Where did the smile go?" and I told him I didn't feel like I should smile.

He said, "Go ahead and smile."

So, I smiled, and he took the picture.

I told him I was suddenly feeling sad for the first time and he said, "Well, then let's go have a drink."

Classic guy response. I laughed.

There was a liquor store across the street where they used to buy cases of Pabst Blue Ribbon. Dave apparently had been a VIP there because he was able to walk right past the warm cases in the store, and instead go into the walk-in box to get cold ones.

We crossed the street and went in through the attached bar, instead of the convenience store entrance. Armando said he had never come in through the bar, so this was a new experience for him – and he thanked me for that. We sat at the bar and ordered PBR in honor of Dave, and talked some more.

I finally said, "Armando, you had to have known he was crazy, right?"

He was quiet for a minute, then he told a story about a time when Dave was posting that he had a gun and was going to kill himself, but warned that if any friends called 911 he would shoot whoever showed up, too. Armando said that Ray called him from California and asked him to go check on Dave. When he got there, he said that Dave opened the door and pointed a toy gun in his face, until he said, "Dave, what are you going to do, shoot me?"

"But that was just Dave," he added.

"But did you know at the time it wasn't a real gun?" I asked.

"No," Armando said, "but I knew Dave would never shoot me. Besides, he didn't own a gun. He was just upset about something."

"That's still not ok," I said.

"But that was just Dave," he said again, and looked at me with a soft smile.

Armando was Dave's friend – he saw the Madness, but chose to focus on the generous friend he knew: The friend who recorded and

122

played in his band, and gave him some of his favorite memories. He saw some of the darkness that I saw, but loved him anyhow.

I took another sip of beer, and thought, *Brother, I certainly hope you're seeing this.*

After we finished the beer, Armando took me to the same Mexican restaurant where he took Dave for his farewell dinner. We sat on the patio, and Armando pointed out the table where he and Dave sat, that final day. I took a selfie with Dave's seat in the background. And I smiled.

Armando had to get going shortly after lunch because he had cousins in town and was going to go out and have actual fun. My words, not his.

I could sense that Dave was lighter.

The next morning, I went to Dave's church.

Lincoln Square Presbyterian Church.

"I could tell you my adventures –
beginning from this morning,"
said Alice a little timidly:
"but it's no use going back to yesterday,
because I was a different person then."

-Lewis Carroll, Alice's Adventures in Wonderland – Chapter 10

On Sunday morning, I headed to Dave's church. It was still so strange to me, the idea that Dave went to a church every Sunday – even if it was ostensibly just to work. I woke up thinking, "Today is going to be the sad day."

I'd spent the first two days speaking with Dave's male friends -but guys don't really talk about their feelings. Being with them was like learning history. Meeting the women who knew him would mean connecting to the feeling of him being gone. It would be more intense.

The front desk called a cab for me. I was headed to Lincoln Square again – this time by myself. I felt nervous.

I knew this was going to be harder than anything I had done, so far.

I am not comfortable in churches – and I am not comfortable talking to strangers. Yet here I was, alone in a cab, heading to a strange church; going to meet new friends who I'd never met before... again.

The cab pulled up in a neighborhood and stopped. The church held its weekly services in a school gymnasium. I got out on faith, assuming the driver had taken me to the correct place. As I walked up the sidewalk, I saw a little church sign… and then I heard music. Live, guitar-band music. I walked toward the sound, as it called me in. I went through the doors and my whole childhood flooded back to me: people singing and playing guitar…. and, out of nowhere I began to cry.

124

Jodee was in the middle of a song but she saw me come in. She must have recognized me from my picture, because she waved to me and smiled from across the room. The rest of the rehearsing band members looked up and smiled at me, as well. I smiled back, through tears – and I could barely speak… I was overcome with emotion.

It all made sense to me in that moment – and now I knew why Dave was there all those years - and I knew he was there, now.

He may have been too young to remember the family get-togethers and the jamborees, but somewhere in his mind this must have seemed like the place where he belonged. To me, it felt like going home.

People came to greet me, with an enthusiasm well beyond politeness. They needed to meet me, as much as I needed to see them. They were grieving, and confused… they wanted to connect.

As church began, I sat in my pew, with my guard down. I was not defensively waiting to be bored and annoyed, as I usually was in church – like at Boy Scout events, or wedding ceremonies. I was open to a message, and the one delivered was spot on.

The sermon was titled: What Does It Profit a Man to Gain the World (to lose or forfeit himself), from Luke 9:18-27.
Pastor Chad began explaining that in this chapter of Luke, we see that Jesus was raising the dead to life, healing the sick, declaring sins forgiven… but, throughout, is the question: Who is this man?

Who is this man? I started to tear up. I related to that question - that was my journey. I tried to focus. I was taking this out of context, and this sermon wasn't about me.

Pastor Chad went on to say that this taps in to a fundamental question that humans have: "What is the life that is worth living?" He said that what Jesus' words invite us to, is a radical new way of thinking about the life worth living. To save your life, you must lose it.

To save your life, you must lose it.

Ouch.

I fidgeted a little in my seat… and the tears started, again. I had felt for a while that my brother had actually gained life by leaving his impaired physiology. The disorder wasn't who he truly was. I was misinterpreting the sermon… but it still felt like the words were meant for me. I knew they weren't, though – that would have been impossible.

Chad said that historically, followers of Jesus have valued generosity and hospitality. And forgiveness. Followers of the teachings of Christ are called upon to set aside grievances.

But, I thought, *Dave was not physiologically able to do that*. Even his spiritual growth would have been restricted by his biological body.

And Chad spoke of original shame – about our nakedness – but said that some of the clothing we seek may be metaphoric… like aptitudes, education, accomplishments…
Ok, that was a little too personal…

I had the overwhelming feeling that God was talking directly to me; that I found myself, again, in front of exactly who I needed to be in front of, when I needed to be in front of them.

The miracle of "church" – whether it's a group led by a pastor, or simply two people connecting in a spiritual moment – seems to be that we will take from the interaction what we need to take from it, as individuals. What someone else took away that day may have been a completely different message.

We all showed up to receive a message that day. Mine was painful.
God had just called me out on hiding behind accomplishments and
degrees…

Chad went on to say that it is by dying to that identity formation that
we sought to hide with, that we may find light. HE knows we have
chased after false loves and false hopes. In dying to ourselves, we
are born anew.

False loves and false hopes. That, I definitely heard….

Was the message that I needed to shake off my attachment to
accomplishments, in order to find light, myself?

Chad said that through Christ we affirm the dignity of our neighbors,
and their value as an image of God. Life is a gift, and the gift is not
for us to keep for ourselves, but to spend for others, that you will
know the final word in your life is grace and resurrection. We are
invited to find life worth living…

I thought of all of the people who had come to me before this point,
to tell me of my brother's generosity…
I became aware that this service was becoming acutely painful for
me. I was now sobbing, but felt physical pain as well.
Then, as if on cue, Chad spoke of how when light comes into
darkness, it is painful. If you are sitting in a dark house, any light
that suddenly comes in through a crack can be as sharp as a knife.
He said that light, in certain situations, can hurt. Salvation may hurt
before it heals.

Double ouch.

The light really was hurting me – and I hadn't realized how dark it
was where I had been.

That day was the most inspirational day of my life. I found the
Church I'd been looking for my whole life. I understood why Dave
was here every Sunday, week after week, doing the sound
engineering. Everything made sense, for the first time in a very,

very long time. The people of the church were wonderful; the sermon was wonderful. Every word Pastor Chad said rang true to me – and it was the first time in my life that I had ever had that experience in a church.

Or maybe, it was the first time I had been open to it.

I sat there with the overwhelming feeling that I was exactly where I was supposed to be; hearing exactly the messages I was supposed to be hearing. I sat there feeling like I had found something that I had been missing, something valued and treasured – but I hadn't known it was gone.

And the realization came over me: I set out to meet Dave, and in the process, I met God.

Had that been the purpose of the journey, all along?

After the service, I was greeted by several people. Their grief was fresh as well, and it seemed to be very healing for them to be able to meet Dave's sister. I looked everyone in the eye as they shook my hand and introduced themselves, trying my hardest to see them, and hear them, and remember everything they were saying.

They loved Dave.

He never missed a church service. He was there every week doing the sound engineering – for a live band as well as the mic audio for the sermon. It was overwhelmingly comforting for me to know he could go there and feel loved and valued every week - and from what the parishioners were telling me, they really did love and value him.

Everyone had nice things to say about Dave. They were eager to share fond memories of him. One woman said that every year she runs the food pantry, and for each of the past two years, Dave had donated 6 hours of recording studio time for her fundraiser. She said he apologized profusely to her for not being able to do that this year, because he was moving. This is why people loved Dave – he was kind and generous when he was not clouded in the borderline darkness.

After church, a few of us went to lunch. A lovely woman named Darla insisted on paying my tab. She told me that she had wanted to treat Dave to lunch before he moved, and regretted that she didn't get the chance. She said she felt that this was a chance to make up for that.

Darla had written Dave a letter after he moved, but became aware of his death before she had a chance to send it to him. She sent it, anyhow, with a note to my parents attached. Many people from the church also sent letters to my parents, after they learned of Dave's passing.

At lunch, I spoke candidly about my brother's struggles with mental illness, and his history of suicide attempts. I wanted to provide these people who cared about him with the clarity they deserved. At one point, his friend Nathan asked, hesitantly, "If you don't mind me asking, what was his diagnosis?"

"He was mostly just misdiagnosed," I answered.

"What was the misdiagnosis?" he asked.

"At one point or another, Dave actually got every diagnosis." I said.

"Wow," said Nathan, "Well, in some ways that just feels right..."

I went on to say that he was actually suffering from something called borderline personality disorder, and that it was a very misunderstood disorder, which usually results in alienating loved ones, misperceiving threats, and multiple suicide attempts.

Everyone listened and nodded as I relayed what I knew, and how it related to the experience of Dave that they had. I knew I was bordering on betraying his privacy, but these were the people who had cleaned up his suicidal messes time after time. Literally. They deserved answers. They needed answers, so they could heal.

I told them all that it was the belief of our family that the church is what kept Dave alive, and without them, he would have been gone years ago.

I asked my new church friends at lunch what their belief was about people who cross over with significant issues... do they have to work through the issues on the other side, or did they cross over clean. They unanimously said that they believed he would have crossed over clean; at peace... That was their faith.

A week prior, I would have rejected that, and considered the unilateral belief to be limited by tradition. Everything I've experienced indicates that we cross over and still have some work to do. But that day, in that moment, good people were honestly answering my question, and I believed them... and more than that, I hoped they were right.

One indication that they were right was how Dave had spoken of the suicide attempt where he was revived, and all he could remember was how peaceful he felt before they brought him back... or pain-free at least... and how horrible it was to be conscious again with all the pain rushing back. Jodee later told me that at that time, they were particularly worried about him getting out of the hospital, because he was still suicidal... and within days he did try to kill himself again.

Jodee was acutely aware of David's dark side. She told me that he was always very sweet and generous with her, but there was one time when he became very angry with her and threatened to end their friendship and never return to church. Someone had asked if the sound connection had been checked, and Dave became enraged. He took it as a personal attack. Jodee was totally caught off guard, but was able to salvage the relationship by not being defensive, and by apologizing until Dave accepted it.

As the pastor's wife, Jodee spent a great deal of time in the church office, which shared a court yard with Dave's apartment and studio. After Dave's wrist-slitting and other suicidal attempts, it was she and

130

some church members who went into his apartment to clean it up, so he wouldn't come home to the horrible scenes he left behind.

After the time Dave returned to his apartment, still suicidal, she said she was keeping an eye on him and she saw smoke billowing out of his apartment. She and another person rushed in and dragged him out. That was the time he had taken a grill inside and tried to asphyxiate himself. She said it was his only sober suicide attempt. When she tried to go back in and turn off the gas, he grabbed her and wouldn't let her go back in because it would be dangerous for her.

His only sober suicide attempt...

He wanted to go back to that place where he felt no pain. There was certainly evidence that he did cross over with no pain - at least, initially. I knew in my heart that the peacefulness didn't last long, as he had asked me for help a few days after passing. He may not still be in pain, but he knew he was still in the dark.

I walked with Jodee back to her house and spoke with her and Chad for quite a while: About Dave. About faith. About scripture. I asked Chad to discuss with me what the church's perspective of suicide was, since there are so many people try to proclaim that those who kill themselves can't go to heaven (Joan's friend was unkind enough to share that sentiment with her shortly after David's suicide, and it broke Joan's heart that a friend would be so cruel to her).

Chad shed some light on where that belief came from. To paraphrase: In an effort to collect money from confessions, the Roman Catholic priests determined levels of sin: taking a life being among the most serious of the mortal sin variety... and through the Catholic tradition, someone who committed suicide would not have had the opportunity to confess that sin or receive last rights. Therefore, they could not crossover free of sin, and could not ascend to heaven.

For the most part, protestants have rejected that concept, believing that Jesus died to wash away those sins, and as such, a Christian's soul would have been cleansed of all sin at the moment he passed.

Chad shared with me that Dave had admitted on several occasions to wanting to die, but lamented that he couldn't overcome the instinct to survive.

The question remains as to whether Dave was at the church just to do sound engineering, or if he enjoyed listening to the sermons, as well. I told them that my guess was that if he had ever heard anything that offended him, he would have walked out and never returned. The fact that he went to that church, faithfully, Sunday after Sunday, year after year, indicates to me that he was listening – and like me that day, found himself not only *not rejecting* the message, but actually hearing it.

Chad visited Dave in the hospital after each suicide attempt. He said that one time, when he was talking to Dave about God, Dave said, "Jesus was a badass." I would agree with him.

The church threw Dave a going away party before he moved back to Florida. It was hosted at Jodee and Chad's house. The highlight of the evening for the adults and children alike was when Dave set an old "beater" guitar on fire and smashed it on the sidewalk – exiting Chicago like a rock star. Someone videoed it, and he posted it on his Facebook page with the following message:

"Retiring a guitar propa!!!
Fun for the entire family!!
Got this guitar
("Beater" would be an understatement)
a few years ago for a recording project.
It served its purpose, served me well.
Time to say goodbye/ send her out in style!!
Thanks to Jodee & Chad For hosting a little "Goodbye" BBQ/ Get together for me, and the entire LSPC family for their kindness & love over these past years—

Honestly don't know where I'd be without them."

After Dave passed, Ray created a black and white still from the video, which he blew up and framed.

After we had all talked for a while, Jodee walked me outside to catch my Uber. She showed me the burn mark that was still there on the sidewalk, in front of her house, from the flaming guitar. I took a picture of it for Ray.

In some way, that "just felt right."

The people from the church knew who Dave truly was. They saw his dark and his light, his goodness and his flaws. And they loved him, anyhow - exactly as Jesus would have postulated. There's nothing more powerful for a sceptic than to seeing people who live the message of Christ. And there's nothing more off-putting then people who just talk about it. I felt like I had been witness to something very powerful that day.

I felt like I saw the existence of God in people – and what can evidence more light than that?

****

Hues of Dave Facebook Post, August 13, 2017

*Me: ... to all those still scratching their heads about Dave,
I can tell you with certainty that the church he did the sound
engineering for, every Sunday for 5 years, is where he belonged.*

*They loved him.
I loved them.
It was a church I've been searching for my whole life.*

I totally get it. They "got" him and loved him anyhow.

*And if he didn't "get" them he would have walked out a long time
ago and never looked back.*

*I have a renewed faith in God and I believe he must have too,
whether he acknowledged it or not.*

****

Every day that I was in Chicago, I walked through Lincoln Park and I was amazed by the gardens. August in Lincoln Park was remarkable, I thought. For three mornings in a row, I greeted the day in the park. On my last morning, I got up early as usual, had some breakfast, and went across the street to Lincoln Park to say goodbye. I started walking through the park, expecting to see the beautiful gardens... but as I looked around, all the flowers were dead.

I walked on, taking pictures of the fields of wilted yellow flowers – which had been in full bloom during the days prior. As I walked, I heard something crying. I followed the sound and saw a squirrel on a tree, screaming at me. I stopped, concerned that it was hurt. It was hanging upside down at a weird angle, body sprawled down the trunk of the tree with a foot, stretched out above it, that seemed to be stuck.

I tried to see if its leg was caught on something, but I couldn't get close enough to the tree. Even if I could have gotten close enough, it would have bit me if I had tried to touch it.

It screamed again. I looked around, but there was no one who could help me. I couldn't leave it there, but I couldn't help it, either. I was stuck – not knowing what to do. The squirrel wasn't squirming; just screaming and hanging there. After a very long time, or what seemed like a very long time, it finally moved.

Thankfully it helped itself, and was able to get loose - and it wasn't suffering anymore. Thankfully... because my worst fear in that moment was that I couldn't help it, and I would not have been able to turn away, and go back up the rabbit hole, not knowing if the poor creature was going to live or die.

I couldn't do that... ever again.

I made my way through the winding paths to the zoo to say goodbye to the lion. But there was no lion: He wasn't there. I thought: how impossible - or just statistically unlikely – that Lincoln Park had been alive and thriving while I was here, and dead on the morning I leave.

Isn't it more likely that I had been sitting at home, instead, this whole time… looking in the mirror; just imagining that the wildlife was responding to my journey.

Clearly, my trip was over. I needed to go back through the looking-glass to home.

*****

After arriving home and unpacking my clothes, a flash of something caught my eye. I looked down and there, at the bottom of my now empty suitcase, was a very shiny dime.

Who the heck is Chuck?

"Well! I've often seen a cat without a grin," thought Alice;
"but a grin without a cat!
It's the most curious thing I ever saw in all my life!"

-Lewis Carroll, Alice's Adventures in Wonderland, Chapter 6

The miracle that manifested after my brother's death was the number of people who came out of the woodwork with love, and compassion, and a desire to help and contribute and understand. Chuck was one of those people that emerged. Apparently, we went to high school together. He knew my friends and I knew his friends, but I had never met him, before Chicago.

He reached out almost immediately after Dave died. He offered to talk with me, any time, and when I decided to go to Chicago, he went out of his way to meet with me. I had asked my friend Cathi about him, since he seemed to come from nowhere, but knew everyone. "Chuck is harmless," she had said, "but I have a strong feeling you need to meet with him for some reason."

Apparently, Chuck lived with Dave and his wife for a short time in Chicago, during the period when Dave was not speaking to his family. Dave and Chuck had run in the same circles since they all lived in Florida, and Dave helped him out with a place to stay when he needed it.

He had very nice things to say about Dave – whose apartment had been full of music and rescue animals.

When we met in Chicago, Chuck told me that he only had one experience where Dave went dark. He stepped on an eggshell and had seen, once, what I had been describing in my posts about borderline personality disorder. He said that Dave's extreme reaction surprised him at the time, but made sense now that he understood what that was. Chuck moved out shortly after the incident with Dave, but kept in touch.

Chuck didn't hold a grudge.

Chuck appeared in this story out of nowhere, and then, just as quickly he disappeared. Off of social media. Off of cell phone grid. No one who I am in contact with knows what has happened to Chuck.

So, where the heck is Chuck?

Like the flowers in Lincoln Park, Chuck was gone. I don't know why I "needed" to meet Chuck, as Cathi put it ... but maybe it was just to evidence that even though people come and go, their light can remain.

A Cheshire cat fading away, leaving only a smiling memory.

Chuck was funny. We ordered sandwiches at the farmer's market. He insisted on paying for mine.... they asked for a name for our order, so he picked, "Elvis."

****

*"Your smile walked out that door
– you don't need me anymore…*

I guess I knew…

I guess I knew."

*-<u>The Walking Smile</u>,
original song by "Claudio"
Recorded at Stray Dog Recording Studios*

****

Chapter Ten
Cheshire Smiles

*"Alice asked the Cheshire Cat, who was sitting in a tree,
"What road do I take?"*

The cat asked, "Where do you want to go?"

"I don't know," Alice answered.

"Then," said the cat, "it really doesn't matter, does it?"

— *Lewis Carroll, Alice's Adventures in Wonderland – Chapter 6*

A few days after I returned home from Chicago, Lucy died. Lucy was my Aussie-mix rescue dog. She was a gentle little dog who kept to herself, but came out happily from wherever she was napping for dinner or a walk.

We found Lucy, lifeless, in the flower garden. My mother had recently taken her to live with them because, according to her, my other dog wouldn't let her eat. Lucy was fat. She was eating just fine. I thought my mom just wanted her because she was so sweet. I recently found out that she took Lucy to her house for David – because he loved her and missed his own dogs. He told her he thought it would help him to have Lucy there. Lucy had recently been diagnosed with congestive heart failure, but the vet thought she had another year.

Years ago, when I noticed Lucy curled up in the back corner of her cage at the dog rescue, I asked to see her. She had her back to the people milling around, nose tucked away in an effort to make it all go away. When they took her out of the cage, I thought she was the prettiest dog I'd ever seen. The beautiful garden of summer blooms was a fitting place for her final rest. She was buried there, among the flowers.

After Lucy died, my mother declared that she and Dad did not want another dog.

I got in touch with the rescue group that I had gotten Lucy from, and asked if they still needed foster volunteers. They were very happy to have me foster dogs who were up for adoption, so they wouldn't have to live in a cage while waiting for a home. The first dog I brought home was named Claus.

Claus never went back to the rescue – my mother adopted him, and changed his name to Chewy, short for Chewbacca. He does look just like Chewbacca – but I know that his Star Wars name was really in honor of David, whether my parents realize that, or not. Chewy is a very loved, and a very loving, little boy.

Sometimes, pets rescue you right back.

Gramma Margaret fostered for ASPCA when she was alive. I used to say that Gramma went to doggie heaven. Cindy said that after Gramma Margaret died, she would find shiny dimes all the time, in very strange places. One time she saw a bright, shiny dime on the middle of the emergency room floor. She felt gramma's presence, and she said that it brought tears to her eyes. Recently, my mother had an epiphany – she said her mother used to tell them to always keep a dime in their pockets, so they could call her.

When he was alive, Dave took in the stray dogs that no one else would want. Most of them I never knew, but I remember that one of his first rescues was a shepherd mix named Gibson. Gibson was hard to look at – part of his jaw was missing, possibly blown off by some low life with a fire cracker. People can do truly evil things.

My mother told me that Dave tried to look into fostering for a rescue group in Chicago after his dogs were taken from him by his ex-wife, but he said that when he went in to apply, they looked at him like he was a piece of garbage. Who's to say if it was his misperception of a neutral face, or if his signature haggard, disheveled, smoking-drinking-musician look turned them off.

In any case, he got angry with them and left.
I hadn't known about his recent attempt to foster. After he passed, one of my regrets was that had I known, I could have set him up with the rescue group here. Fostering a dog may have saved his life, for a while longer.

I continued to foster – a total of three more dogs; each until they were adopted. My son got 120 service hours for helping, which we can use to meet scholarship requirements – and my family got a reprieve from grief, for a while, through giving love to unwanted animals.

Fostering was work – for all of us. A new dog every few weeks meant new training, new schedules, new little faces to miss when they found homes and left our lives for good...

My mom would pick the foster up from my house during the day to come play with Chewy at her house while I was at work, and then I would take them back home in the evening. It meant extra time in my morning routine, and with two boys in high school, I was short on morning time, already. Getting ready for work one morning, I was feeling a little anxious about taking on yet another foster pet, when something flew out of the closet and landed on my foot.

It was a dime.

Gramma Margaret must have been proud of us, looking down from doggy heaven.

Boston Tea Party

She generally gave herself very good advice,
(though she very seldom followed it)…
"But it's no use now," thought poor Alice,
"to pretend to be two people!
Why, there's hardly enough of me left
to make one respectable person!"

-Lewis Carroll, Alice's Adventures in Wonderland, Chapter 1

As I keep saying, the miracle in this story continues to be the people that have come into my life and the gifts they have brought: proof of good in the world, proof that we are all connected through something higher that ourselves… and proof that I am on the right path. These experiences aren't unique to me. They are there for anyone who is open to seeing them.

In November 2017, I was sent to Boston by my company to present at a conference on Alzheimer's Disease. My friend Kelly also attended the conference. She had gone to graduate school in Boston – so everything just seemed to come together for us to find ourselves no longer in Florida, but in Boston, one evening, having dinner with her old friends in the hotel where I was staying.

…which was statistically unlikely.

Kelly introduced me to a lovely couple with two adorable children. I felt so honored to have been invited.

As Kelly spoke with the husband, his wife and I started talking about work and the conference. She asked me what my specialization was in psychology, and I said that I currently did psychological testing for Alzheimer's research, but that my expertise was in autism. And then, for some reason, I told her that I was writing a book on borderline personality disorder, because my brother suffered from BPD, and he had recently killed himself.

I surprised myself by disclosing that – I had been vacillating on whether or not I should write the book. Who was I to tell the story? ...With my crazy pennies flying about... My motivation for actually writing the book had peaked in Wonderland a few months prior, and was starting to falter. I was re-focused on the real world: work, paying bills, college applications and high school drama. My book seemed trivial. My story seemed like a dream from which I had awoken. A fringe reality.

To my surprise, my dinner companion told me that she was connected to a clinic that specializes in the treatment of borderline personality disorder. A light came back on - and I realized how passionate about the topic I really was. We spoke for a while about the disorder; how the prognosis has improved and how the definition of the disorder has changed over the years. I told her what I had learned about the disorder in the months since my brother's death, and she shared insights that she had gained.

I felt, once again, like I was in the right place, at the right time, on the right path. I was engaged in a fascinating discussion about borderline personality disorder, but I was at an Alzheimer's conference. It was unexpected.

After dinner, we all said goodbye in the lobby, and I commented to Kelly how lovely it was to meet her friends. She asked what we had been talking about, and I said that I was sharing my experience with my brother's suicide.

Kelly said, "Well, she is an expert on the disorder - her father is credited with creating the diagnosis."

I was stunned: the woman sitting next to me that evening turned out to be Dr. Gunderson's daughter, the man whose lectures and books I had been pouring over for months since my brother's death. How and why would I have ended up at dinner with her, in Boston of all places – a place I had never been to before? Actually, I know the how and the why: There was something at work in my life to keep me on the path.

144

It was a sign to keep going – to pick up the journey… to finish the story.

It was time to meet Ray.

****

Dave's Stray Dog Recording Studio Post, continued

--- One of my favorite scenarios (that comes up all the time), is when I'm working with a 'new' band: Sometimes, after they do a 'take', or an overdub, or whatever, they'll ask me what I think/ if it was 'good enough'?

...Thing is:

1) What are you asking me for? YOU'RE paying ME to set up the mic's and hit record. Why would you give a fuck what I think?

2) How would I know? I just met you. I've never heard you play this song. I don't know your capabilities...

...So the real/ only answer is self-evident, and always appreciated/ taken in the spirit with which it was intended:

"I don't know. Can you do it better?"

"Yeah."

"Well... There ya go. Do it again, but better. Ready? You're rolling..."

****

****

July 5, 2018

I took out a bottle of red and went to the kitchen to find a corkscrew.

I heard David say, "You've been drinking too much."

"It's wine," I said, "Jesus drank wine."

"Jesus didn't drink wine like you do," he said.

"What, are you friends now?" I said, continuing to uncork the bottle.

And out of nowhere, a penny fell on my foot.

****

A Ray of Light

I heard this analogy recently: you are walking with a cup of coffee, and someone bumps into you and you spill the coffee all over yourself. Why did you spill coffee on yourself? Most people say it's because someone else bumped into you. The reality is: you spilled coffee on yourself because that's what was in your cup. If you had something else in your cup, you would have spilled that.

In other words, those of us striving to be good people focus on our calculated, conscious responses to life events. The question is: what will you spill all over yourself if someone bumps into you?

I started to have an existential crisis. I felt like I wasn't living up to my end of the bargain with God… or the universe… or a higher power… to become a better person and fulfill a higher purpose. Every time I think I'm getting there something happens and coffee spills all over me.

I see posts on David's memorial page. And then another. And another. And then I see a response from Ray. And all of these people who are part of David's journey have now become a part of mine… in my interpretation, the evidence of God working in and among all of us.

148

Yet I felt guilty because these people weren't *supposed* to be in my life. I felt like I was cheating at something – insinuating myself in to friendships that were his, not mine. He never would have introduced any of us in life… but, somehow, he has introduced us, in death.

Ray said once that Dave was a man, and now he's a legend.

What I have experienced on this journey is that once human frailty is gone, all that's left is the essence of the individual. People are revered after death in a way they weren't when they were alive. It seems that after death, all of their earthly flaws fall away, the spirit regains its rightful significance. All that is left is spirit. They are now revere-*able*. They have become their higher self and they return to the higher power, and that's why we truly honor them so much more in death than we were able to in life.

And in that respect, Ray was correct. Dave was now larger than life – the life that limited him through biology.

Ray saw the best of Dave – whether intentionally or not. He remained a person of light to him, because he was always on Dave's side and never confronted him in a way that made Dave feel threatened. He met Dave when he was married, and didn't try to maintain friendships with both people after the divorce. He just stuck by Dave. That was the kind of friend Dave needed, and the only kind of friendship he would have been able to understand.

From what I know of Ray, he is a kind, gentle person. It seems he never *didn't* express an understanding of Dave's side, and he didn't challenge the fundamental ideals behind Dave's perspective - mostly because he enjoyed Dave's humor, which often manifested in sarcasm. Ray enjoyed the banter, and whenever Dave started going dark, Ray went light.

After Dave's death, Ray posted a photo composite of himself and his brother and his cousin, all drinking Pabst Blue Ribbon at the same time, but in different states, in memory of Dave. It was my first exposure to "Ray". Since then, my friends and I sometimes order PBRs – in honor of Dave, who we are only meeting now.

Ray was like an angel to my family after Dave died. He was a rock for us – a touchstone. He was someone Dave's family had never met, yet he was also grieving the loss of a "brother". He answered every question we messaged him, patiently and honestly. We met Ray via social media after Dave died…. And since that time, he had gone above and beyond to be a friend to my family, as he had been to Dave.

After Dave passed and I shared with Ray that all of Dave's belongings were missing from the moving truck, Ray messaged back to say that he and his brother were monitoring the web and craigslist for Dave's missing stuff. He was as heartbroken as we were, of that I was sure.

When Dave's things finally arrived, I was messaging Ray pictures of items as the moving guys were unloading them – to make sure they were really his. He was the one who would know – and he was there on the other end responding to every photo I frantically sent.

My son inherited the guitars and amplifiers. He inherited Dave's signature, self-customized Fender bass. The rest of Dave's sound studio was offered up to Ray and Armando. We finally met Ray in January of 2018, seven months after Dave's death, when Ray and Armando drove down with their cousin to collect Dave's sound engineering equipment.

Meeting them at my parents' house was a surreal experience – for all of us, I imagine. After months of posts, and videos of recording sessions, and listening to the music recorded with my brother in his studio, meeting Ray was like meeting a celebrity.

They didn't have much time to spend in Florida. They were here for a day, just to get the sound equipment, and then they had to head back home. It was a weekend trip and there were work schedules to maintain.

We were all blessed with the opportunity for my dad and son, Aidan, to jam with them, one last time, on Dave's instruments. It all took place in my rec room. We drank PBR and played his original song, "Everybody's Such An Asshole". It was beautiful.

Before he left, I took Ray aside and told him that Dave was communicating with me, and that if there was anyone else Dave would try to communicate with, I believed it would be him… and if there was one method, it would be through technology.

When they left my house after the jam session, my whole family cried. It was our last human connection to Dave…. and we were saying goodbye. Later that week, Ray posted, "Jamming with Dave's family was the most healing thing I have ever taken part in. Thank you… I felt him there."

On June 7, 2018, almost a year after Dave died, a voicemail popped up on Ray's phone. It was a message from Dave – but it was from two years prior. Ray posted the screen shot and the voice recording on Facebook, writing:

> "How did this voicemail go unnoticed for almost 2 years??? I found it 15 mins ago!!! A tiny little gift to me, from David. I'm sharing the wealth with all of you as this will be a tough week."

No one could hear the message when they clicked on it, however.

Finally, after several responses, Ray apologized and said he had no idea why no one else was able to hear it. I had an idea, however, and I responded: "Because the message was just for you, and he's pissed off that you're sharing it!"

I wasn't joking. That entire scenario was totally and utterly Dave of that, I have no doubt.

Ray and I interacted fairly consistently in the year following my brother's death.

When Ray accidentally lost all of Dave's music, I was able to make a recording and send him a USB drive with the all of the songs that, ironically, Ray had originally sent me.

Ray was awesome, and I told him so.

He said, "Thanks Pamela, you're pretty awesome yourself."

I am awesome.

So, why wasn't I awesome to Dave?

I withheld my light from Dave… just as he withheld from me.

Now my outpouring of awesomeness showers Dave's friends... where was this me when he was alive?   Darkness is so strong. Like coffee. Like tar.

I am beginning to wonder if Dave ever saw the best version of me? I can't remember a time when he did. I can't remember a time when he would have. The best version of me shrunk away from that darkness. The darkness brought out the darkness in me. The same way the darkness brought out the darkness in him.

So, if I had been the one who died, what would he have written about me?

I once asked Ray if he wanted me to use his real name in the book. Ray paused a minute, then told me that he knows that other people had experienced a dark side of Dave, but that he never had. He expressed concern about not wanting to participate in a part of the book that would disparage his friend, and I respect that. I don't want to disparage his friend, either.

At the same time, borderline personality disorder killed my little brother, David… just like it will kill 10% of the people who have it , while the rest of them just suffer, and wreak havoc on the lives of everyone around them.

I reminded him that Dave tried to kill himself numerous times, and each time was prefaced with drama and documented in his own social media posts. There were countless public Facebook rants - not just posts that were limited to his friends. For years, Dave had been screaming out that he was in pain. He wanted everyone to know how much he suffered, when he was alive. So, I would argue that I'm honoring that by telling the story of what we know about how much pain he was in… and why.

As I have said, borderline personality disorder killed my brother. He certainly was a borderline – but he was primarily and fundamentally, still Dave. Dave had a disorder, but *he* wasn't the disorder.

He became the disorder when the darkness shrouded him… but Ray only saw Dave, because Dave only saw Ray as light.

Dave's story deserves to be told: He struggled and died for this story to be told. He bled and screamed for this story to be told.

Ray thought about it and said to me:
"If he is going to be Dave in the book, then I want to be Ray."

And that's why Ray was, and is, light.

Also, Ray wants Antonio Banderas to play him in the movie.

****

7/4/18

"Any messages for Ray?" I asked?

*Dave says that he did send that voicemail message to Ray –
It really was him.*

*In fact, Dave says, he sends Ray
electronic messages all the time,
but Ray doesn't trust his instincts that it really is Dave.*

*Dave also said that he sent a message to Armando,
by messing with something (technology?)
but Armando thought it was the cat.*

Dave thought that was funny.

"I'll have to ask Armando about that," I said.

"No, don't," Dave said, "it's funnier this way."

****

Ever-vacillating between wanting to write this book, and fighting exhaustion and self-doubt, I reached out to my cousin, Carol. I knew what his friends thought about me telling the story, they were mostly supportive, and thankful for the insight... but what did family think?

Carol sent me the following message:

> "Pam, this is your journey as well as David's, through your eyes. It takes a ton of courage to put yourself out there, vulnerable to others' criticism, as well as their praise.
>
> But do it.
>
> Do it for all that you've learned so far and the unknown knowledge that is waiting. I believe with all my heart that this story needs to be told.
>
> Go forward, warrior."

It's not just new people I was meeting. It was the people who have been in my life forever that I was getting to know in a whole new way. I had known Carol all my life as a kind and gentle person. I now knew her as a sage.

One year after David's death, I finally met his college roommate, Pam. Ironically, the person who lived geographically closest to me was the last person I went to meet. It only took me 20 minutes to drive to her side of town. We had become friends on Facebook – connected by loss.

I enjoyed her posts, but wouldn't have thought we had too much in common, considering she was a lifelong friend of the brother who I thought I had nothing in common with.

I pulled into the little strip mall where the restaurant she had chosen to meet was located. It was in an area of town I was unfamiliar with, even though I've lived here for 30 years.

This is my 50th trip around the sun. I have friends, I have family, I have things I like to do, and I am busy... but in my journey this past year, I have discovered new places and new friends - friends who have been in my periphery for 30 years, yet whom I never would have met, on my former path.

My journey to meet his friends had taken me full circle, back to Orlando. I had lost touch with who my brother was... all I saw at the end was a dark, crazy person; someone you couldn't reach.

I was almost relieved when Pam told me that the general consensus of his long-time high school and college friends was that Dave had really gone off the deep end. They had all been very concerned about him, for the past few years. So, I wasn't Mad, after all. I drank the beer I had in front of me and the world returned to normal size.

Pam said she found out Dave died when some mutual friends, who had fallen by the wayside, posted that they had lost "one of their own." She said her immediate response was anger – and said she lashed out because these people who were posting had lost touch with Dave years ago. They had walked away.

Pam called them two-faced.

She told me that she had felt angry with these people who suddenly cared about Dave again, when they had abandoned ship a long time ago. It's hard for people in the trenches to watch others just give it lip service – so I didn't tell her that I was probably like those people. I thought I was done with him, too... fed up with the crazy war and the landmines. But when the war was over, I still mourned the casualties. Their grief may have been more genuine than she realized.

Pam said that his friends saw him deteriorate significantly after his divorce. His college friends were collectively not fond of the relationship, and never were terribly close to his wife. According to Pam, Dave tended to attach to people who would enable his Madness.

156

She and Dave reconnected on Facebook several years ago. When he reconnected with my parents and visited Orlando once or twice a year, Pam was able to meet up with him, along with a former roommate of his. She echoed his former bandmate Brian's assessment that Dave had not seemed to have evolved at all from the musician party kid he was in 1990.

According to Pam, Brian, loved Dave like a brother. She said he was more hurt by Dave than angry with him. He was angry because of Dave's lashing out against him. She said that Brian hadn't chosen sides between Dave and his ex after the divorce - Brian "wanted to be Switzerland."

When she said that, I knew that Dave would have perceived neutral as hostile. If you weren't 100 percent on his side, he would have perceived you as against him.

Pam said that Dave actually called her once and told her that Brian was spying on him. She said she just laughed and said, "Dave are you hearing what you're saying? Say that out loud: 'Brian's spying on you.' Why would he spy you?"

She said Dave just laughed and dropped the subject. She hadn't realized at the time how serious he was. The borderline paranoia had set in, prompted by some perceived slight - but because she was kind to him and non-threatening, Dave did not turn on her. He apparently did not distort her interactions with him, because he did not perceive her as hostile. He wasn't psychotic or incapable of rational thought – but when he was in primal threat mode, there was no logic in that space.

Pam and I started talking about the trip to Iceland she had recently taken with her teenage son, to see the Northern Lights. Then she surprised me by saying she had been impressed that I had gone to Chicago by myself to meet Dave's friends. She said she couldn't believe it when she saw my Facebook posts. I was stunned that a recent world traveler would be impressed by my little Chicago trip.

Apparently, she knows what it's like to be on a journey… she gets it. She took her son to see the Northern Lights… she's a fellow warrior.

By the end of our lunch, I realized that Dave's old friend and I had more in common than I had imagined.

EVERYBODY'S SUCH AN ASSHOLE

Some-times   I   think   there's a   bet-   ter   place   waiting   A place
In the   midst   of   all   the   bullshit   and   stu-   pidity   that

where   all   good   deeds   are re-   warded
The   feelings   stick   like   velcro

but sur-   rounded   by   schmucks   and an-   noying   Mother   Fuckers
And when the news   is   always   bad   news

My good   will   be-   gins   to e-   rode
Seeing   good thru the   evil   is seeing a   diamond through the   coal

It's like trying to be a   Vulcan   in a   world   full   of   Klingons
I'm   trying to be a   Cartwright   in a   world   full   of   horse thieves

AND IT'S HARD   SO   HARD   WHEN   EVERYBODY'S   SUCH   AN   ASSHOLE

1

Chapter Eleven
Return to Wonderland
(Second City, Second Wind)

"I think I could, if only I knew how to begin."
For, you see, so many out-of-the-way things had happened lately,
that Alice had begun to think that
very few things indeed were really impossible.

-Lewis Carroll, Alice's Adventures in Wonderland - Chapter 1

What I have learned, above all else, is that despite the fact that I love my brother's song, everybody's actually *not* an asshole. I found the light in my brother's life – the light he couldn't see: good people who showed him love, even though it drained out faster than anyone could pour it in.

My brother killed himself in a time of political polarization in this country; a time when the media is trying to convince us all that we are enemies... brother-against-brother, civil war caliber enemies... protesting and threatening and shooting things up. However, in the midst of all this polarity I find that people are just trying to do the best they can.

Most of us actually have the same values, fundamentally. It appears we align to different poles on a linear scale, but I think, instead, the scale wraps around as a circle - with a central value system. Though shalt not kill. Do unto others. Help the suffering. The central belief system in America radiates out to different places on the circle but it still comes from the central value system - and central to all of the chaos is that our people are fundamentally good. One asshole shoots up a school and there are a thousand helpers and a million people brought to their knees in grief or prayer.

Almost one year after my first visit, I found myself again in Chicago, this time with my son, Aidan. We stayed in Lincoln Park, at the hotel with the rooftop bar, and I showed him around the park to the zoo.

Aidan and I went to Lincoln Square Presbyterian Church service on a rainy Sunday morning. The cab pulled up to the curb outside of the school where the church met every week. We paused a moment, trying to visually locate a door, and navigate the quickest pathway through the rain. As we were getting out of the cab, the driver suddenly said, "Wait," and handed me an umbrella.

Light.

Being at the church gave me a sense of communion. It felt like coming home to old friends. It was welcoming. Darla was there – she said she hadn't been able to attend service since we last met, for a variety of reasons, but she came to see us and was so glad to be back among the congregation.

They still missed Dave. The church was a safe place for him. He could be as authentic self, there, because it was not a place that caused him to feel threatened.

Once again, I went to lunch with a group after the service. I told them that my mother wants to meet everyone, someday, but she still does not feel like she is able to make the trip, emotionally. My new friend Gina said that whenever my Mom is ready to come to their church, she is welcome.

We spoke about how healing it has been, for all of us, that we were able to meet. Gina said that after Dave killed himself, she had been left to wonder why they hadn't been "enough" to keep him alive – why they couldn't keep him from feeling so empty. She had initially felt like they had failed him, and she had been struggling with that. Meeting me and hearing about the disorder helped her to understand the situation a little better… and she said it truly was healing.

I had been able to help them on the journey through their loss, as they were able to help me on my journey through mine. These people had meant so much to me; I was happy to hear that I had given back to them.

The reality is that my brother was eventually going to kill himself. That doesn't mean that the time spent with him was wasted or not valuable. We are all going to die – but that doesn't make us less valuable to each other, today. Dave was eventually going to kill himself, but that doesn't mean that all of the time he spent with the church was wasted or meaningless.

He lived as long as he did because of them: That is an accomplishment, not a failure.

After lunch, we took our now-annual selfie; this time, with Aidan included. Next time, I hope my mom is in the picture, too.

Darla generously offered to walk us around Lincoln Square, so that Aidan could see Dave's studio. The old church office was boarded up, and the whole lot was under construction. It would have been unrecognizable, except there, on the gate, was the Stray Dog Recording Studio sticker and the handwritten note to the postman regarding package delivery, yellowed and tattered by time.

I took a picture of the gate with my phone, to preserve the last mementoes of Dave in Chicago. We started to walk away, but Aidan stopped and went back to the gate – he slowly and carefully removed the fragile note and Stray Dog sticker. Darla had a book with her that she was intending to give me, and we tucked the treasures carefully between the pages, so they would not crumble into dust. The book, as it turned out, had been written by Darla's sister, about her own journey.

Many people have asked me what Dave's perspective of an afterlife was, given that he was suicidal for so many years. The answer is: I would have no idea what he believed before he died. He had been going to church for years, albeit as a sound technician and not necessarily as a parishioner. We do know that he heard the sermons, and I know that the people of the church hope he believed - because they would hope he was able to cross over into heaven. It would have been part of their belief system that faith would have gotten him there. I would say that if he truly rejected their belief system, he would have walked out the door and never returned. People who actually live their faith are inspirational – and he was surrounded by them.

I met Jodee for breakfast a few days later. She had been out of town on a tour promoting her new CD that Sunday, and wasn't able to join us for lunch after church. Her original album had been recorded at Stray Dog, and she and Dave had been close. When I was at lunch with the church people, the story of Jodee pulling Dave out of the smoke-filled building was revisited. It was a true story, but at the same time, it was also a metaphor. She pulled him out of a burning building more times than she probably knew.

At lunch, Gina had said, "Jodee is a warrior." I just smiled.

A fellow warrior…

I know that if I ask "Alexa" (Amazon Echo) to play a song by Jodee, it does – it plays the album recorded at Dave's studio. I also know that Jodee tours around the country, playing her original songs. In my eyes, she's definitely a warrior.

Jodee said that she would be touring with another singer, Laura, and that they would like to come to Orlando to meet Dave's parents when they are in Florida. Laura also recorded a CD at Stray Dog – she had won the session in one of the charity auctions Dave donated to.

We looked at our calendars and the only date they were available was October 12th.

Dave's birthday.

****

On this second trip to the second city, I was able to connect with Armando, who, once again, took time away from his busy life to meet up with me. He arranged for me to see the new studio that they were setting up with Dave's sound engineering equipment. He took me to his friend Marcos' house, where the new studio would be.

Last year, Marcos' mother-in-law died, about same time as Dave. He inherited a house and sound equipment, and he seemed to be very humbled by these gifts. He told me that he wants to pay it forward. Part of Dave's mission statement was that everyone should have access to record their music, and it "just felt right" that the studio ended up in these hands.

Marcos said that he thinks maybe, since his mother in law and Dave crossed over at the same time, they may have met on the other side and arranged this. Considering everything I had experienced this year, I wouldn't disallow for that.

Before I left, I warned them both that Dave messes with technology. Marcos said that he'd recently had a tech glitch with the sound equipment that he couldn't work through - and it wasn't making any sense – but it resolved itself instantly when he reached out to Ray and Armando.

I said, "Then that was Dave."

After the studio, Armando and I went to another rooftop bar: This one had a skeleton revolving on a motorcycle. And so ended another surreal and wonderful visit to Chicago.

Dear friends, clients, comrades,

For Starters:
Thanks all for the love and support throughout the years !!!

It appears that my Landlord is intending to sell the property at 4910 N Lincoln, where SDRC currently resides, possibly as early as this September. Any potential buyer will most likely tear down everything, and put up some brand new, oh-so-necessary additional condos in the area.
(Basically, I'll be out of here, I have no idea where I'll end up).

I currently don't have any plans/ whatever to move and renovate a new place into a use-able recording facility by myself: I'm this much older, and weaker than I was when I constructed this current space from what was basically a garage into a professional recording environment.

Point is: If you have any projects currently in progress, or anything in the plans for recording with me, I suggest you get on it in time to finish sometime this summer/ before this fall and book something/ get on it!!

Anyways… If this is it:

Nothin' but love from this end!! Think I'm really proud of what I've done: Lots of great memories working with some un-believably talented artists, Made some good friends, and got to enjoy the company of all-fucking-kinds of folks that I never would have otherwise. Yeah, it's true: Folks is mostly just folks (Whatever hue/ color, accent, fashion-sense, musical taste, all that shit)…

OK,

Thanks,
d-
Engineer, Stray Dog Recording Company

Chapter Twelve
Eggshells

"When I use a word,"
Humpty Dumpty said, in a rather scornful tone,
"it means just what I choose it to mean - neither more nor less."

"The question is," said Alice,
"whether you can make words mean so many different things."

Lewis Carroll, Through the Looking Glass – Chapter 6

I do understand now, why when someone dies they are put on a pedestal... or at least thought of in a different way. It's because their soul is now free from their mortal imperfections. They are now light. They cross-over and they're no longer limited to what they were, here on earth – and somehow, our spiritual selves recognize that. They are remembered and revered because the soul is revere-able. Honoring someone that died is honoring God. This why Dave can be more himself in death than he was in life. Because he is. We all are. We become fully who we are when we shuffle off this mortal coil4.

Borderlines are souls trapped in bodies that physiologically disconnect them from the light. They can see the light in other people – and when they do, they're fine. But due to physiology, they can quickly, and irrationally, perceive that someone has bad intent - and suddenly they lose touch with that light in the other person. And they may never see it, again.

To a borderline, you can't be a good person with a flaw. You can't be a good person who hurt them. You are light, or you are dark. There's no gray area.

I "friended" Dave once, on Facebook, a few years before he died. It was during a time when my parents seemed to think he was coming

out of the depths of the darkness. We were Facebook friends for one day, and then he unfriended me.
He sent me a message saying that he didn't want me to see his posts.

After revisiting the past year, I had an epiphany. Maybe he didn't hate me. Maybe he wasn't keeping himself separate from me because of dislike for me – maybe it was because of dislike for himself. Is it possible that he just didn't want me to see him for what he had become? It had never occurred to me that I was that relevant to him, until he reached out from the other side.

This book was written to honor my brother's life – and the battle he finally lost. To write this book dishonestly would have been a travesty. The whole story needed to be told, if any of it was told. And the truth is that in life, I saw him as an emotional hijacker. I saw him as someone who hurt my parents and destroyed everything around him. I saw him as someone who hated me for no reason and blew me off his path along time ago – and for 25 years I felt angry and defensive.

In the end, I had no compassion for what he was going through, because he seemed to be doing it to himself. The disorder is one of pathological selfishness – manifested because of physiological defensiveness.

Not all borderlines will kill themselves, but most will try. Some will succeed, whether inadvertently or not, and eventually one of the I'll-show-you suicidal gestures will be lethal.

Not all borderlines alienate everyone around them, but they all will feel like they did. And they will feel a profound sense of emptiness.

They will suffer and those who care about them will suffer.

Borderlines are not always crazy. They are not psychotic (psychotics can't not be psychotic), but borderlines appear psychotic when they are in that irrational place, triggered by someone stepping on an eggshell. When they perceive an attack, they go crazy - but when they are able to see the light in someone, they can be their best self – because, in their mind, that person actually deserves their best self.

Unfortunately, due to increased frontal lobe damage (from drugs or years of perceived threat) my brother was deteriorating to the point where his best self was seen less and less frequently, and by fewer and fewer people. Because of misperceived threat and disordered thinking, my brother lost touch with his family for many years. He reconnected with my parents, eventually, but he and I really never did. For the last 25 years I did not know the man he had become-and I barely remembered little boy I grew up with.

I set off to meet the brother I didn't know, and in the process, I was reconnected to the brother I had lost.

After a year spent meeting Dave, this is what I learned:

Dave was a very sensitive individual. He was affected and often incapacitated by perceived slights and injustices. He was surrounded by people who loved him and cared about him, but he couldn't feel it. It was like there was a hole in him, and no matter how much love and caring was poured in, it just ran through and left him empty.

As a result, he felt profoundly lonely and isolated. These feelings made him angry and resentful. He often acted out on those feelings. He was compelled to retaliate against perceived slights and injustices. The darker he became, and the more people he alienated, the worse he felt about himself.

And on more days than not, he really did want to die.

He knew what he was doing, and often articulated that he hated himself - but even when he acknowledged an over-reaction, he still couldn't quite own it. His reactions were ultimately in response to someone else's behavior, in his mind. His disorder was one of distorted perceptions; of feeling like a victim and perceiving abuse where there was none intended.

On the flip side, if you had not "hurt" him or violated his trust (again his perception) he would do anything for you. He was a fiercely loyal friend. His extreme sensitivity also made him extremely charitable and giving with those he trusted.

He was a gifted musician – described to me by more than one person as a musical genius, particularly in sound engineering - but he did not feel that his talent was appreciated, which further contributed to his feelings of loneliness and resentment.

He was extremely intelligent, and quick witted, and funny. His humor had an edge, though, and the line between joking and snapping was often blurred. One had to typically walk on eggshells around him. That was part of the disorder.

Finally, he cherished animals. He rescued dogs that no one else would want and gave them affection that they may never have gotten if it weren't for him. He truly loved and valued them, and they could provide continuous unconditional love in a way that humans could not.

The loss of his dogs was probably a bigger tragedy for him than most of us can comprehend. That vast emptiness, and the hole through which all feelings of connectedness just drained out of him, could be constantly filled by the adoration of his dogs.

Once they were gone, the emptiness began to truly consume him...

Sensitives don't make it very far in this world. The loss that so many people felt after he died was real - so much of what he had offer the world is now gone forever.

My son recently graduated from high school and told me that he wants to get into sound engineering. I felt my heart crack.

I felt that intolerable panic of "too late."

My son never got to have a conversation with his Uncle Dave about that. He'll never get to learn from the master who was at one time within his reach.

All of that genius and creativity is resolved to a pile of ash.

A short time after Dave died, I stumbled upon this post from Quentin. He was responding to someone else's post, a few months after the suicide:

> *"This David thing has really put a toll on my life. I started school last Thursday and I visited some of my old teachers. They all said I seem to be less of that happy kid I was last year or something to that effect. I don't raise my hand in class as much and I'm not very social with my classmates at all. Like Joan once said, they don't know what we're going through. It's one of those things where you're not purposefully doing it, but it just happens that way. Anyways, thought I'd tell you because you seem to be taking it pretty hard too."*

Borderline personality disorder wreaked havoc on our family.

I believe that people who commit suicide have lived beyond their threshold of pain for a long time, and they simply can't take it anymore. I believe it would be selfish of us to ask them to.

I loved my dog, Maggie, so much that I put her down. I gave the directive to let her go in the middle of surgery, when they discovered that she was full of cancer – because the vet advised me that it was the kinder thing to do. Stitching her up and bringing her home just to suffer and die a painful death at home wasn't something I was going to do to her. I afforded her more empathy and dignity than that. I loved her too much to bring her home, just to selfishly hold her until I was ready to say goodbye. I let her go to spare her suffering, because I loved her, and I have to live with that.

We let David go. Looking back, maybe the signs were there this last time - but the signs were always there. This time, he didn't fire a warning shot - and this time, nobody stopped him. We finally gave him the freedom to go, because we loved him. And we have to live with that.

I haven't told my parents this, but during my interactions with Dave since he passed, I have gotten the distinct impression of dying of thirst. The official cause of death was overdose – he had apparently crushed several acetaminophen/codeine tablets and ingested them – and they were probably crushed for fast absorption. After a previous overdose attempt, he'd had his stomach pumped, and was revived. He would have known better this time.

The coroner reported that he died on Thursday, which was the day he was found - but my mother and I knew instinctively that he had passed away on Wednesday. No one had heard from him since Monday night, however, and after Monday, I could no longer feel the darkness. Ray and I believe that if he had been conscious, he would have reached out to someone after Monday. I believe he was in a coma, starting Monday night. I believe he was aware of being thirsty, and passed away on the third day of his coma – quite possibly from dehydration.

The bottom line is that he was angry and in a borderline rage when he left my parents' house that Monday - and in a blur of rage and retaliation and knee jerk reactions, my brother killed himself.

Borderlines are impulsive in their reactions - but did he mean to die? Ray doesn't think so, because Dave didn't fire a warning shot this time. This time there were no dramatic calls – he just left a message for Ray sometime that evening, saying hello in a way he always had.

He was reckless at the very least. Over-medicating himself to numb the pain, and not caring if it killed him, would be something he would do. Ray may be correct – this may not have been a result of a desire to die as much as a result of not caring if he lived. The end result was the same: Dave killed himself.

Then, a few days later, my brother reached out to me and said, "It's dark here."

I told him that he was supposed to go into the light, and he said that there was no light. He asked me to help him see it, and through my year-long journey through the looking glass, I've seen more light in people than I've ever seen in my life. I've seen people at their best, shining from within. The light within us exists, and it is real, and it is tangible.

When people have the opportunity to shine and they do, that's the light of a higher power in each of us. The church people shone with it. His friends shone with it. My friends and coworkers shone with it. All, exactly when I needed them to...

He asked me to help him, so I set off to try.

My cousin had perceived him at the beach, with a sense of relief and peace, immediately following his passing.

I felt him in the dark, in need of help finding the light.

I'd like to believe that he really was at the beach, and that the call to help came from within me... from my own inner darkness that needed to be enlightened. Either way, the call set into motion a series of meetings and events that changed me forever. Time is a human construct. What came first and what came later may not exist in the spiritual realm.

He said he was in darkness – and since then he has also said that my cousin's dream was right: he *was* on the beach. It's possible that both scenarios happened simultaneously in the spiritual realm, and a year apart on my time.

All I know is, he was with me on this journey. As I was able to see the light, I believe he was able to see the light. And I think he finally made it.

In the end, it's only a passing thing, the shadow. Even darkness must pass. A new day will come. And when the sun shines, it'll shine out the clearer. Those were the stories that stay with you; that meant something.[5]

I wish you peace my brother. *Namaste.*

****

During this journey, I have believed as many as 6 impossible things:

1. I believed that PBR was actually pretty good beer.

2. I believed that sometimes, some of us hold up a beacon, intentionally or unintentionally, that allows for communication from the other side.

3. I believed that when we pass on, darkness eventually falls away, and all that's remains is light.

4. I believed that there is a spiritual connection among people, and that we will be drawn together at the right place in the right time, when we need to be, to learn what we need to learn, if we are open to the experience.

5. I believed that despite the statistical unlikeliness of any of these events happening, they did.

6. I believed that I could help my brother find the light.

****

****

Things Dave has told me in the past year:

- *He said that when you cross over the energy goes with you. It dissipates initially, but then it comes back, and you have to work things out.*

- *He said not to spend our lives sad and grieving over his death. There is nothing to regret - drugs killed most of the pain, anyhow.*

- *He said he's sorry, Dad. He says he was an "asshole" and you didn't deserve it. He says you were his best friend.*

- *He said, "I'm ok now, and I wasn't before."*

- *He said that he didn't intend to kill himself this time, but he didn't care if he died.*

- *He said that Cindy's dream was right. He did feel like he finally made it. He was on the beach with his friend when she went back to the hotel to grieve him after he died.*

- *He said that he hears the music that we all write. He loves it. He hears my Dad's songs dedicated to him. He is humbled, surprised... and touched.*

- *He says he likes the new dogs. He says that they don't bark at him, anymore.*

****

The End

"What is the use of a book,"
thought Alice,
"without pictures or conversations?'"

— *Lewis Carroll, Alice's Adventures in wonderland Chapter 1*

"This book is going to be about the discovery," my friend Allie said to me one day, "It's how you came from one thought process and moved over here."

About a week after Dave died, I met my friend Brian at Disney Springs. It was a typical Florida summer deluge, so I waited for him in an art gallery, where I was drawn to an artist's alternative rendition of Alice in Wonderland.

Alice was sitting alone in a garden in front of a castle gate, with an open book on her lap. To her left was the fading smile of a cat, and behind her was the white rabbit preparing to signal an event with a trumpet. White roses, partially painted red, were at her feet. And way in the distance, barely visible, sat Humpty Dumpty, teetering on a wall.

When Brian arrived, we ran across to the restaurant and sat outside on the covered patio listening to music. The grief was still very fresh, for both of us, so we ordered PBR in honor of Dave, as his friends had done.

At the end of the day, before we left, Brian went into the gallery and bought me that painting of Alice. I hung it on the wall on my dressing room when my dad and Aidan finished the remodel of my bedroom. Every day for the past year, I have looked at Alice looking back at me, both of us knowing that Humpty Dumpty eventually would fall... and that all the king's horses and all the king's men would never be able to put him together again.

It's been over a year since my brother died. Aidan has started college. He came home the first weekend, stopped by to have dinner and pick up some things, and on his way out the door asked his little brother if he would like to come back to the dorm and spend the night with him on campus.

Quentin was thrilled. Watching them go off together, I thought about my little brother coming to stay with me on weekends, when I went away to college. I did have a brother, once - and then suddenly, he was gone.

There was only one part of this story that wasn't entirely true. There was one other person at the funeral home: the friend who had taken him to the beach; the last person to see him alive. She didn't want me to write this book. She said it made her sad to think that negative things would be said about him, and that she only wanted to be part of it if the book was about his music.

So, out of respect for her, I left her out of the story. She was a big part of it, though – and my family cares about her, very much. I want her to know that Dave's spirit is no longer trapped by physiology. From everything I have experienced, he wanted the story told. He has been part of this journey – and, together, we have found light.

After all this time, I finally found out what it was that triggered that last, fatal fight between Dave and my dad. I discovered the grievous injury that launched my brother into his final suicidal rampage: The morning after the moving truck arrived and my brother's stuff had not been on it, my dad and he were calmly sitting in the living room, and my dad made an offhand, sympathetic comment, thinking about the chaos and upset of the day before:

He said, "Those poor drivers."

Egg shell cracked.

<u>Epilogue:</u>

My friend Christine is an editor.
She moved away shortly after Dave died,
but offered to edit my book when it was written.

After a year of writing,
I contacted her to see if she was still willing to help me
and read my work with an editing eye.

She said: Of course, she would help!

I told her that the caveat was: I needed her feedback in two weeks.

I wanted to coincide the book launch with Jodee's visit:
My brother's birthday.

I set a goal... the clock was ticking.
A friend offered me her wine bar as a venue.
People were RSVPing. His old friends were coming in.

It was going to be a celebration.

Christine came through, and spent hours with me on the phone going
through the manuscript which she had printed out on paper,
old-school style.

At one point, I stopped her and said,
"I feel guilty that you are putting so much time and effort in to this."

And she said, "No, you feel blessed."

References:

American Psychiatric Association. (2000). Diagnostic and statistical manual of mental disorders: **DSM-IV**-TR. Washington, DC: American Psychiatric Association.

American Psychiatric Association. (2013). *Diagnostic and statistical manual of mental disorders* (5th ed.). Arlington, VA: American Psychiatric Publishing.

Akiskal HS, Chen SE, Davis GC, Puzantian VR, Kashgarian M, Bolinger JM. (1985). Borderline: an adjective in search of a noun. Journal of Clinical Psychiatry. 1985;46:41–48.

An Interview with John Gunderson on Borderline Personality Disorder by Signume Karterud in Oslo, Norway. (Video copyright UiO 2015). Retrieved June 1, 2018 from https://www.youtube.com/watch?v=neSKp4hSesM.

Berenson, K. R., Downey, G., Rafaeli, E., Coifman, K., & Leventhal, N. (2011). The Rejection-Rage Contingency in Borderline Personality Disorder. *Journal of Abnormal Psychology, 120*(3), 681–690.

Donegan et al (December 2003). *Amygdala hyperreactivity in borderline personality disorder: implications for emotional dysregulation.* Biological Psychiatry, Volume 54, Issue 11, Pages 1284-1293.

Gunderson, John G. and Hoffman, Perry D. (2005). *Understanding and Treating Borderline Personality Disorder: A Guide for Professionals and Families.* American Psychiatric Publishing, Washington DC.

Gunderson, John G. (2009). Borderline Personality Disorder: Ontogeny of a Diagnosis. *The American Journal of Psychiatry, 166*(5), 530–539.

Gunderson, John G. et. Al. (2011). *Family Study of Borderline Personality Disorder and Its Sectors of Psychopathology.* Arch Gen Psychiatry. 2011;68(7):753-762.

Hoffman, P. (2003). *"If Only We Had Known",* National Education Alliance for Borderline Personality Disorder Presentation, Powerpoint. Retrieved July 1, 2018 from https://www.borderlinepersonalitydisorder.com/wp-content/uploads/2011/12/If-Only-We-Had-Known.pdf

Kriesman, J. and Straus, H. (1991). *I hate you--don't leave me: understanding the borderline personality.* New York, Avon.

Linehan, Marsha (1987). *Dialectical Behavioral Therapy for Borderline Personality Disorder.* Bulletin of the Menninger Clinic, 51(3) 261-276. The Menninger Foundation.

Mason, P. T., & Kreger, R. (2010). *Stop walking on eggshells: Taking your life back when someone you care about has borderline personality disorder* (2nd ed.). Oakland, Calif.: New Harbinger Publications.

May, Jennifer et.al. (2016). *Dialectical behavioral therapy as a treatment for borderline personality disorder.* Mental Health Clinician: March 2016, Vol 6. No. 2, pp 62-67.

Nasrallah, Henry A. (2014). Borderline personality disorder is a heritable brain disease, CURRENT PSYCHIATRY April;13(4):19-20, 32.

National Institute of Mental Health (2018). *Borderline Personality Disorder.* Retrieved June 1, 2018 from https://www.nimh.nih.gov/ health/topics/borderline-personality-disorder/index.shtml.

New, A., Triebwasser, J. and Charney D. (2008). *The Case for Shifting Borderline Personality Disorder to Axis I.* Biological Psychiatry.

Redmayne, Kevin (2015). *It's All In Your Head: Borderline Personality Disorder and the Brain.* Blog: Articles on mental health and international development May 23, 2015.

Scotton, Bruce (1996). Introduction and definition of transpersonal psychiatry, in Textbook Of Transpersonal Psychiatry And Psychology. Basic Books, New York.

Weill Cornell Medical Center. (2007). *Brain Abnormalities Underlying Key Element Of Borderline Personality Disorder Identified.* ScienceDaily. December 27, 2007.

Zanarini, Mary, et.al. (1997). *Reported Pathological Childhood Experiences Associated with the Development of Borderline Personality Disorder.* American Journal of Psychiatry 154:8.

Footnotes:

1. Lyric from White Rabbit, by Jefferson Airplane (1967).

2. Obi-Wan Kenobi, Star Wars movie, 1977.

3. The Cage. Travis (2001) *The Invisible Band.* Sony

4. From William Shakespeare. *Hamlet.* 3rd soliloquy, Act III, Scene 1.

5. New Line Home Entertainment (2003). *The lord of the rings.* Jackson, P. et.al. Los Angeles, CA: New Line Home Entertainment. Adapted from Tolkien, J. R. R. *The two towers: Being the second part of The lord of the rings.*

Namaste: the light in me honors the light in you

Post Script: The Book Launch Party

Jodee did come to Florida, and performed with Laura on Dave's birthday, October 12, 2018. My friend Mary let me use her beautiful venue at Wekiva Island for the party. Almost everyone who was in the book was in attendance: the whole cast of characters, from a story that spanned decades. Bridges were mended and hearts were healed.

And I know Dave was there:

On the morning of the party, Quentin and I went to Cracker Barrel for breakfast. All of a sudden, Quentin heard a noise and looked down. There, on the floor, was a shiny penny.

Made in the USA
Coppell, TX
29 December 2019